Mind and Itself

Established – July 2025 — October 2025

New York, NY
United States of America
© 2025 Baruch Menache
All rights reserved.
Published by McWest & Associates
ISBN: 978-1-971928-30-2

Mind and Itself

Belief, Civilization, and the Disavowal of Consciousness

Baruch Menache

PART 1: MIND AND ITSELF

Chapter One: Three Degenerative Beliefs of Mind

Section One: Degenerative Beliefs of Consciousness: An Overview

There are two primary beliefs for a degeneration of consciousness, at least for the psychological and ethical implications, or to be more precise: proper procedure in accordance with the functionality of the psyche in reference to its fundamental parameters. The first is the belief in 'magical thinking' (Freud) or the supremacy of thought, which is considered to be altogether otherworldly, to the extent that it cannot be discussed as a process or function and rather succeeds all discussion. The second is the self-identification of consciousness. The third belief is considered normative function with the most limited degeneration.i

The first belief is such that as long as an individual is privy to embodying their experience of life, it is inevitable that something will be believed to hold supremacy, to which embodiment is enabled. Supremacy allows for the influx of information that surrounds a subject, such that it guarantees both continued resilience in stimulating the disciplines and the allocation away from that role of supremacy. Although viewed from the vantage of a subject, where supremacy is overshadowing, in the objective observation, supremacy is a role that takes part in the process of the subject.

When we concern ourselves with the consequences of the mind, the foremost belief about the occurrences of the mind is that they are enabled based on its innate substrate, to which we have no access and indeed to which we are subservient. Such is to be considered pronounced dependency rather than general subservience. To be subservient, there are three elements: one, a hierarchical chain; two, the uppermost echelon of the hierarchy stands above the subject of subservience; and three, the subject is defeated by their status of subservience. If any of these three are not met, it would not be termed subservience. Proclaimed subservience is a case where the subject does not seek to depart from the subjectification, thereby removing themselves from the chain of the hierarchy, placed rather in a state of self-perpetuation.

The second belief associated with such supremacy is the allocation away from personhood, which is the scientific happenstance of the mind, not as a first-person cognitive function, but rather as an organ study to which one has no influence. This is the belief that the mind is so delineated as an organ that we must conjure its most detailed orientation, that of the brain, to which it can be dissected to its details and concluding its organization; all without the premise of a user or recipient of that organ.

The finality of such a belief is merely the adherence to the commencing sociality which such science is dependent, for science is only a discipline of a civilized tradition, and sociality is the format for civilization, thereby having sociality as its most significant aspect. Thus, the hierarchical chain of this format of supremacy is an attachment to a social order, rather than anything related to the individual.

This is finally the belief that current sociality dictates the terms of the organ termed 'the brain', based on the evolution of this sociality, which will determine the conformance and situational assessment of its function. Differing from magical thinking, which is the concealment of the mysterious notion of the mind's happenstance, this is the belief that sociality is as functional as an organization that it should dictate the terms and parameters of the happenstance of the mind.

We acknowledge this by the very terminology in utilizing the word 'brain,' when 'mind' produces the same effect, especially if we are studying the practical ramifications alongside the psychological aspects. Yet, the usage of the word denotes the external formation of the organ, not as something subjectively denoted, but objectively, as one who sees the other, and notes a 'brain,' not a mind. The sociality embedded in the term is transparent. We cannot dictate a form of sociality around and in concern of a 'mind,' for such implies a dynamic function of subject and object, to which the objective is the only claim of reality for any sociality.

The moment we move to communal affairs, we do not have the luxury of subjective mood points, since it would lose general movement among constituents. If we are to consider a single mind and its personal occurrences, then we cannot consider another being along that continuum. The subjective vantage point can consider another person, yet this is not a formation of society, but rather the extent of relation between one subjective modality in contrast to the objective view of another.

If we follow the supposition to its comprehensive analysis, we will see that the mind is believed in the same manner as magical thinking, meaning that the intention of delineating sociality to execute the construct of the mind as an organic brain is for the deterrence from recognizing the functionality of the subjective identification with the mind, but more so because it is still believed that the mind is somehow magical and sacred to broach upon. In some ways, we arrive full circle, where magical thinking is thus again taken hold, but only with a deterrence. In the antiquated case, the deterrence was the spiritual leader, and in this case, it is general sociality and specifically those who conjure the details of such while using the backdrop of a scientific discipline.

We must keep in mind, in the case of discipline, as the word denotes, it is a form of disciplined thinking that is part of a broader spectrum of knowledge. In this case, the spectrum is sociality and not knowledge. It is possible to retain a discipline part and parcel of the spectrum of all knowledge, but that would require the removal of sociality as the dominant force of civilization, which seems improbable. When the scientist dictates the parameters of the brain, they are really demonstrating the exemplification of sociality, to which these methods are the terms of such in its detailed formation. If anxiety is a concern, the scientist will dictate the brain's formation of such, so as to form a continued alliance of sociality as the performer of the construct called the brain, but more importantly, the retention of the sanctimonious nature of subjective usage of the mind, much like how a computer holds the user sanctimonious despite its prevailing ability.

Scientists follow a regimen of success in their detailed analysis, but they are merely exemplifying a social need of postulating the brain as an objective form to avoid the subjective identification with thinking as a controlled and regulating function. The success is arbitrary to the objective, which, although could be thought to enjoin in discovery, is laden with the socialized process as its chief aim.

The third belief of the mind is not based on the mystical nature of its innate process, or of sociality that creates a construct for it, albeit with scientific accuracy, but rather that is a subjective function that can introspect upon itself. Meaning, it is identified as a computer that could utilize not only its process but possibly its core contents itself. The mind itself is then utilized as a mind for the capacity of its own nature and its functionality. This does not invoke the belief in the otherworldliness of magical thinking, nor of sociality and its construct that is invoked upon the mind, but rather relies on its inherent nature to produce its identification, which is most like a computer process rather than the other two.

If there is a superior identification to thought processes and regulation, then one will not be able to utilize those tools. Even as there is a sociality that functions as an explication of the process of the mind, to which one can move about in the psyche world to align with that premise, it is of no correlation with the initial psyche enabler; as if somehow the psychological construction has come to be without any determining factor to retract upon.

We could say the burden of supremacy lies in the psyche construction, by its virtue of being sound to the environment, which differs from the happenstance of mind. As if to say, this is real while the other is not, when of course, standards for real and unreal are based on the realm of psyche identification. This then reaches back to the first premise, an adherence to sociality which utilizes the demanding requisite of something real to constitute its structural base, when in fact all along, it is a regulator for the objective of divergence from promoting thought processes to be magical.

Although we have set the premise that self-identification of thought processes is a core evaluation of its utilization, we could find another coinciding contribution. This is the perspective upon consciousness itself, that although it does not make itself known as a substantiated orientation, it can be assured that most will contain a deep-rooted perspective upon its construct.

There are many ways to explain how the process of thinking should occur, some to be most natural, while others to be most unnatural. And with such argumentation, much arrangement of the mind has been made in the intentionality of a direction that presupposes this analysis. Therefore, it is imperative to make an analysis known so as to avoid the assumption of a single characteristic of thought which is dominant solely based on its most natural sequence of the psyche, or in the way the mind was 'meant' to be.

Most of civilization, and surely preceding it, there was a manner of psyche usage which has been a catalyst to a certain version, especially as a hunter-gatherer which surely was not concerned with mind's utilization, and can be a criteria of what constitutes natural thinking. This form of thinking has the psyche itself present its contents based on a conscious imprint of memory, which recycles memory for the majority of a lifetime.

This is why family-based institutions were prevalent from ancient times with most fervent veracity, making the assumption that somehow family and familial bonds are the significant element of existence. The familial body did not just serve its domesticated properties, but more so for its source of original conscious imprint, which was utilized to be recycled over and over, until one had fulfilled the full spectrum of adulthood under that criteria.

It would seem that the adherence to a familial body lies with the presupposition that the conscious imprint was aligned with the figures who brought such to bear. If the mother was both an individualized persona and the source of consciousness, it is no wonder that the next supposition is that one requires the maintenance of such figures throughout one's life, and consequently without any alteration.

They are the bearers of consciousness, to which all later memory serves as its basis. This supposition is both the cause of parental dominance, to which, by exerting control and regulation, they are viewed by the offspring as parameters of existence to which deviation is not possible. The irony is that such figures are both viewed as this rigid formulation of character and dominance, while also as the proprietors of consciousness, despite these two aspects unable to follow the same process. If it were an experience of consciousness, then it was not formulated and set by distinct parameters, and if it were not, then there would be no lasting effect.

In this way, overtly domineering parental figures do not gain a foothold, since it becomes a habitat of limited consciousness. When we study the psyche of the infantile mind, we will notice that the source of the consciousness was not upon the direct interaction of parental dominance, but rather despite it. They were merely marionettes in the cosmic influence of consciousness, to which they are spectators for the psyche from the very beginning. They become associated as a bonded formation, as would be expected, for the infantile mind does not have the engineering of the mind to perform a distinction. Yet, it is resting upon the figures themselves to provoke an awareness of that inherent distinction, and failure to do so lies with the very supposition of the parents in assuming they are the bearers of consciousness rather than marionettes of the environment.

The very fact that there was a switch in their lifetime, from first viewing their respective parents as the bearers of consciousness to then concluding that that instead of their parents being the torch carriers, they have matured to be such through adulation. In this way, the child never gains the knowledge of that separation, for an immense lineage has determined that from parent to child, they were the beholders of consciousness, rather than marionettes in the process. Once the child matures, they only need to retract their entire supposition of childhood to recognize the clear indications of separation.

Yet, we do seem to inaugurate an adherence to a memory-based lifestyle, not for the natural circumstance of psyche process but despite it. If consciousness is separate from specific figures, which in fact it is, then a perspective that controls the psyche process on such a basis is also false. This does not change the fact of tradition and memory as a stabilization to consciousness experience, but it is not the objective of continuing psyche behavior but rather as a computer to which storage is a necessity for later extraction but not the objective of the function of computing, which is to compute. In the case of the psyche, it is to receive data from perception unaltered by the memory.

We can begin the analysis to what gain would an existential existence, for the mere continued data stream and computing process, just as we seem to view the computer as existentially threatening had it itself been experiencing its subjectivity. However, we must first utilize the psyche in a proper manner that it was meant to perform and only then can we broach upon existential inquiry into the seeming endlessness of a direct and unaltered data stream.

In a sense, the supposition of memory offers a semblance of home for the psyche, for now there is ownership of existence despite the very real development that memory is simply prior simulated perceptual data. That is to say, memory-based experience is a simulated psyche process, but even more than in a simulation, it is an aggregate of perceptual data that has not retained its original form. Unlike a computer, to which storage maintains the exact copy of the original computation, the psyche cannot retain the original copy. Well, not exactly, for the direct consciousness experience is a direct copy, and if accessed properly, would be akin to having the perceptual experience once again.

This is why hallucinogens can affect perceptual data, for the extraction of memory has been so effective that the general psyche does not have an awareness of current perceptual data and its memory. However, the specifics which ascend from memory to ascertain perceptual dominance is based on a direct correlation of consciousness. The general state of memory is convoluted, to which there is a mixture of associations and consciousness material, which because of its aggregation, does not produce the same effect of perceptual data. It is the same as it was if one properly directed memory, but it functions to avoid performing as such because it seeks to retain the notion of being a memory-based system. In the case of the computer, we can find the same occurrence. The difference between memory and regular computing is only because of allocation in resources, and within all the substrata of memory lies a database of computing that, if allocated, can begin computing in an instant.

In a sense, we can psychoanalyze the hunter-gatherer as being a repetition of the former memory that constitutes their entire existence, which truly makes each day redundant without perceptual change to the psyche.

Perception will only change where it is allowed freedom to receive information despite the criteria of the psyche. But in the case of recycled memory process, all perceptual data is already filtered according to that memory procedure, and no new data is forthcoming. As such, their existence is a mirror of itself. Psychologically, we can determine the lifespan of a hunter-gatherer to be days instead of years, for which those days were the determinants of the psyche, to which the other days merely repeated its imprints without deviation or nuance, or at least not enough deviation to consider an individual lifespan a growth pattern.

The lag of growth in accordance with civilization is the due effect of this outcome. But by sheer population and generational changes began a deviation that we can consider, psychologically, as a development of the psyche, where it was not only recycled momentary imprints of consciousness but a continuous arc of consciousness exposure. But this was a collective effort among a span of diverse people and populations. We could even consider, again psychologically, that all this could have accumulated by a few individuals, but instead was buffered because of this pattern of thought.

Now, let us consider: if perception is not allowed its task and rather must be subservient to memory, would this be the natural mode of the psyche? If we were to dictate that memory is the core function of the psyche, to which all others must adhere, in what way should a historical precedent of individuality take the helm of direction; despite it being based on parameters that are no longer existent in the environment?

If we assume that, based on the lifestyle of the hunter-gatherer, they would be most availed to not disrupt the natural psyche process, and thus it is natural whether we understand a thing or not, we can then follow the mammalian. Does the mammal utilize perception in its congruent form or in its laden memory-centric form? We would assume that memory is all that the mammal works upon, so much so that they remain all but the same generation after generation. If new information were received in perceptual course, we would notice the change from its prior generation. So both mammals and antiquated humans were following this process, yet we are to claim that the contrary supposition is most natural?

The entire definition of what is natural becomes a pressing question. If we dictate that eating food is a natural process, we are conveying in what way we have already experienced that process, not that somehow we generated a formidable study of the design of nature. It is natural because it has followed a proven sequence of history; so in some ways we are invoking that same memory and circumstance. What is natural is entrenched in memory, and what is unnatural is novel and not based on a historical or biospherical precedent.

We notice this in contemporary discourse, especially in the medical field, which contains the concept of a natural remedy; under analysis, this is based on a tradition of what antiquated humans would have utilized. There is nothing less natural about a plastic object than a ceramic one, except that the former has less human interference and thereby novelty. We might assume that anything constructed by the mind, which would otherwise not be found, constitutes the unnatural. Then agriculture would be on that list, for it was an invention of the mind that would otherwise have remained dormant, as well as cooking food, for instance, or any other evolutionary development.

Plastic is unnatural when we invoke the term to constitute memory versus novelty, where plastic does not contain a lineage of memory like that of ceramic. However, we may say, in such usage of the term, that what is most "unnatural" is thus most distant from memory, thereby most readily available to perception in real time rather than reclassified memory. In the case of ceramic, the chosen utilization is mostly invoked from a tradition of memory rather than a perception-based conception, although that depends on the individual.

We find, then, that the most unnatural pattern of thought is one that utilizes its subjective properties and manipulates its performance like a computer contained by itself. If the objective concept is most unnatural, thus least reliant on memory, then we have before us a case where one should subjectively manipulate the device of the mind to be congruent with the most developmental stage of its performance.

Yet we also acknowledge that memory or tradition is crucial to any degree of deviation. An unpredictable usage of the mind would produce an outcome that, in its most extreme, is a heavy state of psychosis. Once we offer the handle of the subjective mind as the ownership of the individual, then all possibility is available, whether good or bad, high performance or detrimental performance.

However, such argumentation, and very much the justification of sociality in gatekeeping such a precedent, is achieved by placing the identification of the subjective mind into the hands of social tradition and its objectivity more than its final research. Yet we can also recognize that disparaging social behavior arises from many sources, and a well-functioning mind is not foremost among them. On the contrary, all forms of social misbehavior, whether in war or within domestic life, are manifestations of the mind's improper use. This occurs not because the mind is bound by the limits of its own subjectivity, but precisely because it lacks such self-awareness.

We may attribute a small degree of social misbehavior to an individual's subjectivity gone awry; however, the greater issue lies in the insufficient regulation of that subjectivity, which leads to frustration within that social environment. We can agree that social performance should determine the extent to which an individual regulates the mind's subjectivity. Since most wars arise from a lack of access, whether to resources, understanding, or opportunity, this awareness should guide our course of direction.

This begins the journey to decipher who is the determinant of mind-happenstance: the one who has a subjective understanding of it, or those who follow its terms and conditions without innate awareness. The aspect of the mind's construction that differs from the natural environment is that its requirement for natural usage is based on subjective circumstance. The only purpose of the mind is its subjective circumstance, as it enables a process that has a greater effect on the biological experience than biology alone.

If a civilization, group, or individual chooses to view the mind as otherworldly, or most worldly and thus not subjective, then the mind will not follow its most natural sequence but rather its happenstance within its environment. If the environment is such a determinant factor for psyche stance, it is almost as if we have allocated the psyche process, in lieu of its subjective power, to become an environmental regulation. In this case, a change in environment would result in a change in psyche, and the regulation of the environment would regulate the psyche. Most importantly, a disruptive environment will disrupt the psyche.

It is not that we have proportionally allocated the consequence of psyche processes, but rather that we have placed it upon the burden of an environment that carries the same detriments and determinants. This occurs only because it is collectively entranced, which leads to a different supposition. If detriment is collective or individualistic, it would not be a notable matter for psyche breakdown, but rather simply a case of more minds gone astray set against fewer.

In the case of environmental growth and development, even if we attribute it to the performance of a perfected regulation of the psyche, that growth is externally stimulated and thus not imprinted upon the psyche. Instead, it relies on the current movement of sociality. When sociality changes, the psyche changes along with it. In some sense, this is a retracted version of the commencement of civilization. Instead of psyche development following an individualistic arc, it relies on the collective to either fall into detriment or succeed in psyche development. If the collective follows the correct string of memories, willing to let go of memory in accordance with perception and its raw form, and to maintain the proper formations of a corrected psyche, then the collective develops, if it does not, the collective fails.

However, it is not the collective or the offering of individual minds for collective aggregation that causes this growth or detriment. Rather, it is based on specific individuals who deviate enough to input growth or detriment. Therefore, the entire collective is redundant and objectiveless. Although it mediates the existential burden of subjectification of the psyche by experiencing the conformity of memory through collective behavior, it is existentially risk-averse and relies on the simulated effects of memory to escape its reality.

In some sense, the entire notion of having the collective unit perform the deed of individualized psyche processes is destined for its own detriment. If the collective is most in search of existential protection, it is most reliant on memory to provide that protection. Thus, the entire collective would enter a stage where memory-based experience is most sought after, and current perceptual data is least available. If existential willingness and availability existed for deconstructing memory and existentially divorcing from it, then in the first place the collective would not be required to gather around this notion, as it adds nothing to the process. The only thing the collective offers is the formation of existential protection, more so, a simulated effect. If that is not the most sought-after element, then individuals would be available to their own perceptual data in lieu of collective aggregation.

We are not discussing the overall nature of collective organization or its objective, but rather the specific notion of the identification of minds and the identification of consciousness.

Another questionable justification for the identification of consciousness is not for the sake of its vitality, but for the complexification involved in enabling a procedure, a stream, of consciousness, rather than the encapsulation of a specific time frame of it. In the case of a small encapsulation, one avoids the entire process of the psyche. It is as if one chooses to live in the memory portion of a computer to avoid the computational process that requires a very tight, first-pace, and complex understanding.

Residing in memory and its prior computation is a safe way to avoid complex analysis of the procedure of mind, and also of one's sociality. It is the choice to remain simple in light of the complications that arise with consciousness. However, this is a fruitless pursuit, for the very reason that they are vulnerable to any movement in computation. Having allocated themselves to exist only in memory, whatever computation surrounds them will eventually permeate their memory base and control the entirety of the stance of their psyche, to which they have no remedy.

Unless one chooses to avoid civilization altogether, where it would then be possible to avoid the permeation of consciousness or general computation from the collective, it follows that they will be controlled and regulated by the environment without choice or the possibility of change. Moreover, they do not even have the tools to understand how to navigate the environment, for the very reason that they cannot understand it. They lack regulation between themselves and the environment, and their perceptual data is based on suppositions derived from an antiquated memory base.

They must make coherent decisions about environmental interaction that would be beneficial for their stance within their psyche, though they have no awareness of the true environment, nor the ability to regulate whatever permeation the environment happens to impose upon them. It could be any situation in which a measure of consciousness enters their perceptual sphere without regulation and thus controls their entire platform of memory, without their ever having the tools to move within that memory.

One needs access to computation in order to control memory. Without it, memory stagnates in its aggregated form, moved only by computation and the environmental realm, but in no way possessing a subjective mechanism for controlling or regulating even memory itself, which is the entire basis of their psyche happenstance.

Still, such a justification requires evidence, and it is noticed in the political realm through examples of individualized subjectifications of psyches that have gone awry, proving detrimental to even enter that domain. It is as if one becomes suspicious of all computation simply because some computation leads to detrimental social outcomes (which, of course, it does). Instead, they discard the entire formation of computation as a detrimental procedure of experience.

Moreover, the very memory they rely upon was originally produced through computation. In denying that source, they deny the substrate of their own experience, dictating that its origin is unreliable and unjustified. The fathering of their entire psyche framework is thus denigrated as a possibility of unreliability, making it unavailable for interaction, despite the fact that their entire experience depends on that very source and process.

Although we notice that identification with consciousness can arise from many suppositions, vitality, avoidance of complexification, avoidance of unreliability, avoidance of dependency, there is also the element of seeking the safest possible existence. One may, in fact, believe that consciousness does not deserve to die, that it is immortal in its supposition and substrate.

It is this perspective that leads one to protect consciousness, as if it needs protecting, because of its supposedly deserving immortal nature. Similar to how the Greeks viewed intellectuality as the only element of existence that is immortal, they act on the belief that this immortal nature deserves to remain so.ii

This is ironic, because to protect something immortal is a paradox. If it is immortal, it requires no protection. If it is mortal, it cannot be protected. Because consciousness is not individualistic, it does have a certain immortal property, but it is not the individuals who possess this property. Rather, it belongs to its natural criteria.

Section Six: Vitality, Consciousness, and Existential Function of Intellectuality

Why would an individual, common group, or civilization view consciousness based on the forbearers of its substance, rather than on the agreement that it presupposes individualistic notions? Rather, it is permeable and not confined to domestic affairs, but is itself a supposition, one that renders all domestic affairs subjects of inquiry and purpose.

As we have already noted: if the parental figure does not perceive a general perspective in which consciousness resides within themselves as a proprietorship rather than as a permeable aspect, then the child will inherit that same supposition. In a general sense, this perspective is taken on from other intentionalities, especially that of the vitality that accompanies conscious experience.

Since vitality is something one enjoys, for they are existentially demarcated, and to which vitality is the great remedy, it follows that a perspective arises regarding the preservation of that vitality for what lies ahead. Having noticed a general ascendancy of vitality, one seeks to retain its formation, and thus begins to claim ownership over conscious experience in order to preserve that instant. It is this very intention that drives one to repeat a memory, to continue the stream of vitality in its perpetual motion, and thereby to live a life of vitalization.

However, if one were to take notice of vitality, they would see its contrast, or rather its supposition, as a mere biological jolt of simulated effects against the true existential state. Or, in contemporary cases where the chemical source is recognized, it appears as though a being merely undergoes chemical attendance, rather than experiencing a vitality inherent in the nature of its being.

The reason one chooses to encapsulate that specific vitality is precisely because they believe that vitality, as a notion, is the most realistic mode of existence, placing the burden of proof upon existential disruption. When in fact, upon deeper analysis, one would notice that vitality is simply a simulating effect that alleviates the general existence of non-existence. It is not the fundamental framework, but rather a deviation that may offer momentary respite, yet is not truest to its nature.

In this case, vitality is viewed possessively only because one has not reckoned with their existential nature or understood their existence in a profound or reflective manner. This is why any form of intellectual development eventually recedes into a natural supposition toward the idea of vitality as mere chemical substance, or as substrates not necessarily bound to reality itself, because the intellectual process makes one aware of their existential condition.

We cannot form a coherent, developed intellectual individual who fully identifies with vitality, and usually, the same is true for consciousness itself. Intellectual development inherently challenges prior assumptions and enables movement between different streams of consciousness by its very nature, revealing that consciousness is permeable and not fixed.

It is not the intellectual content that supports this supposition, but rather the discourse and the availability of contesting ideas that drive development, necessitating a disengagement from identification with intellectual suppositions, and instead prompting identification with the consciousness associated with those suppositions.

This is the existential function of intellectuality, more so than the specific content it produces, which may either succeed or fail in terms of sociality. It is the individualized development of intellectual process that enables one to form a perspective on vitality and consciousness congruent with the realistic nature of the psyche. In a sense, intellectuality grants a subconscious awareness of the psyche's processes, and therefore remedies opposing notions of sociality.

Chapter Two: The Process of Perception

Section One: Perceptual Forms and the Animation of Consciousness

A perceptual form in and of itself is considered an actualization of the psyche. To be clear, there is no compartment of the psyche that is labeled consciousness, while other realms are labeled regular sociality. We use these terms to create a theoretical framework, and in a more scientific sense, it should be termed perceptual forms and non-perceptual forms.

Consciousness is synonymous with perceptual forms because they are both attracted to the same source, namely, reality as it is, devoid of social or individual interaction. There can be a perceptual form that is not consciously bound, just as there could be consciousness that is not a perceptual form. Memory, for example, of a perceptual form is not a perceptual form but merely a memory; however, as far as consciousness goes, it is animated as such, and in the re-attachment of that memory, it would be a conscious experience.

This is how we can assume that a simulation in which one is entrenched in memory, even if not realized as memory, would constitute a full social experience, missing nothing, especially consciousness. The simulatory experience would constitute consciousness despite its parameter of reality being fabricated, despite the fact that a simulatory experience will not offer a perceptual form. We may assume it to be a perceptual form and thus conclude that a perceived assumption is as similar as a genuine perceptual form; however, the entire experience is based on memory, whether internal or external, and memory is not perception. If we ever reach a scientific capacity in which the application of simulation is possible, it would be attached to the memory regions more so than any other because it would be applying a modality as if it were present experience. We can acknowledge the familiar narrative arc of such imagination, in which the protagonist somehow meets genuine perceptual form, or one adjacent to it, only to question the state of their memory.

The reason that perceptual forms do not constitute a full conscious experience is in how the ascendency toward that perceptual form was activated. Mammals will naturally experience their state via perceptual forms, however devoid of a conscious experience. The lens which reaches toward the perceptual form is in how one ascends, and that ascension will decide the level of consciousness. Another factor that contributes to the consciousness within a perceptual form is objective consciousness of that form. We can all agree that anything human or social-based will be filled with more imbuement of consciousness than that of an inanimate object. One who spends a long interval in nature may experience, more often than not, perceptual forms, yet with a wading sense of consciousness. The objects of nature themselves imbue much less conscious sentiment than their human counterparts. Beside the philosophical argument that what is most like the source will reanimate itself, so that a human in the face of another human will access consciousness more so than what is dissimilar, we must agree that there is an objective accounting for perceptual forms in relation to consciousness. In the case of ascendency, for example, the child, although filled with perceptual forms, because there is little data preceding the experience of the perceptual form, that object in itself will not explain its extrapolation, and once the experience is over, it no longer constitutes a perceptual form. What occurs in the case of apt ascendency is that the foreground of domesticated development or nuance will be applied to the newfangled perceptual form, which now will be activated in itself based on that extrapolation; all the while, the domesticated development has now been converted into a perceptual form.

After the fact, one contains a memory of the perceptual form as well as its embedded consciousness, which can be retracted to both serve consciousness dissemination but also to the effect of offering that original domesticated data from the vantage of a perceptual form. Instead, this time, the data has not been a procurement of the mind separate from objective consciousness and perceptual data, and is now being served from that realm; as if nature herself is offering back that data, like a tree or a mammal filled with that domesticated sentiment, which is experienced by the psyche as both genuine and true in all its angles.

We notice how we exemplify this process by having children or a pet, which become embedded with our developing aspect of psyche by way of projection, to then have the child or pet react to that sentiment, so that we retrieve the data that was originally private to the psyche, which animates in a fully formed being. There is a perceptual form in the way of a new entity, which can then serve to back stream the original domesticated content but now as a perceptual form with an agreement of sociality and objective nature, and no longer constituted as private sociality of the psyche. This is the ideation of the process we are now discussing, but in realistic terms, it usually does not occur in this streamlined manner because of various obstacles.

First, one must construct a private realm of domesticated content that is not connected, per se, to objective reality, which, if it was, is only an elaboration of objective themes, and not innovation or personal development.

Second, the developing data must be brought upon the object—child or pet—in a manner in which they embody that sentiment without a direct lineage back to the individual. If it seems involuntary or distributed based on a superego imprint they will not react to the sentiment from a differing entity, but only to the involuntary state of being under the authority of oneself. One's psyche will not agree that the final sentiment to which they exemplify is, in fact, a perceptual form, but only a reaction to that involuntary state and not an innovative entity with the accession of nature's reality.

Third, when the entity is re-experienced as differing and thus constituted as a perceptual form, one must retract that sentiment without their original attachment to the domesticated data of the original sentiment. This is because it would only continue the domesticated conversation, offering a degree of nuance or validation. It is only when one is not existentially bound to that sentiment that it can now be retrieved as a perceptual form that has no relationship to their private realm.

The reason psyche elements are scalable is that at each stage, they are predecessors to the next stage, and embedded in each stage are the preceding stages, and to be somewhat philosophical, all succeeding stages. This means that all patterns of thought are one and the same, and only as a format of complexity are they differentiated. In this way, complexity is not a form of differentiation, but rather a form of scale, and we admit this most readily in the complexity of images or documents. If one says something is complex, it means that it follows the same pattern of thinking, only in more detail, more analysis, and on a larger scale. The entire premise of the complexities cannot be found in its preliminary layers unless one were to scale it appropriately. That being said, we may want to assert that not only are psyche elements in this respect a matter of scale rather than differentiation, but it might be the case that most of nature has the same attributes.

Firstly, we must recognize that many of the topics we would like to research, such as political functions or identity relations, are conceptual constructs in the balance of the psyche process, and therefore considerable in their scale. Such that the political entity is the scaled version of the parental figures, and identity formation is a scalable version of the personal realm contrasted with the perceptual realm.

The rest of nature can be considered idly from a psyche stance, where any engagement with reality would be based on the psyche's interpretation. If we constitute a tree or a bush as a possible function from its former stage, it is only due to the psyche's interpretation, such that foliage is the exemplification of Earth or the skillful version of Earth. This is parallelel to the biblical narrative and many other ancient myths about the process of nature.

However, if we were to inquire outside the psyche realm, we must first ask: What is the basis of this realm from which we platform to inquire, if not the psyche? We know such things are possible in a general sense, for there is a scientific process that reaches into a realm freestanding from psyche's happenstance and becomes evidentiary. For instance, an atom has been evidently proven to exist, despite never having received evidence in respect to the personal realm, and even a picture manufactured of an atom is not considered an accurate piece of evidence.

The question becomes: Is the scalable version of that realm governed by the same strictness as the process of the psyche? The answer might be worth inquiring, especially in the realm of science, to determine if such a constitution exists in nature, where an atom is a scalable version of its predecessor in addition to its succeeding progenitor. However, we can never ask this question from a scientific vantage point since we are viewing the basis of an element of study without its adjacent relations. We cannot constitute what the relationship between atoms are, other than in respect to their scientific function. Therefore, we do not have the properties to understand if, in fact, one thing is scalable to another in an intuitive sense, as we would say that the political function is a scalable version of the parental figure.

The reason we understand the political function as a skillful version of the parental figure is not because we have studied the lineage between the two, but because we intuitively understand the compartmentalization of the psyche. Thus, we recognize that the process of the political function is the complexification of the parental figure. We cannot view an atom as the complexification of something proceeding it because we do not understand in what way the atom holds a complexification for a proceeding layer, other than our objective view, rather than the subjective experience of its concurrence.

That is not to say that there is no process of scaling and complexification in its subjective state, but rather, we have no access to its experience as we do for psyche processes. If we were to come up with a scientific method to garner an objective understanding of objective reality that is beyond the psyche's interpretation, and thus find its complexified version and determine if it is scalable, then we would have reached a new era in the philosophy of science.

Once we do get that understanding, we can follow an entire procedure of science where we can almost perceive it in its psychological format, as we would understand the political function as a scalable version of the parental figure. This would mark a future of the psychology of science, not as a psyche process, but rather as an objective psychological process. This would not only be a new era in science but also a new procedure in science.

The problem with the entire thesis of dictating that objective reality is scalable, despite its psyche connection, is that one begins the process of speculation in how their interpretative system will parallel by sequence. We could say, for instance, that a scalable predecessor of a building is stone or Earth, yet there is no scientific substantiation between the materials of a building and the property of Earth, which are compounded elements of various forms and processes, no different than a gathering of differing atoms in a positional form.

Alternatively, there is a direct sequence between the ground and the building, such that we would not even constitute such as a building but rather a formation from the ground onward in a molded process. Despite the human endeavor that generated that process, it can still be considered a cohort of the ground, such that it would not be considered a building. Once the building is constructed, it is no longer considered a social build, but rather part of a structure, or more so, part of nature as it spirits. The social element is simply our recognition of distinguished properties between those who have social endeavors and those who do not. Although this is simply our reconfiguration of processes, from the perspective of objective nature, the building is not a building but rather a compounding of continuous sequences in nature.

In this way, we have just elaborated two themes, both on opposite ends of the spectrum, which do not allow us to admit the proceeding scalable version of a building as the manifestation of Earth. However, with certain parallels to the psyche process, we can admit that there is some lineage of scale between earth and the building, although we constantly remain in a state of speculation. Similarly, in psychology, we demonstrate that the successor of the parental figure is the political entity. All the while, it is not completely accurate to say that one is an indirect continuation of the other, but rather, it has properties that have been complexified to the next stage.

There is something characteristically unique about each level of scale that does not allow a complete attachment to its lineage between levels of complexification. Thus, it is not the foremost process of the revered tactic, but rather a psychological approach to the psyche. One cannot simply discuss the psyche in its current stage as a complexification of psychological clichés, reducing a complex, mature individual to various simplistic processes. Although these processes are attained throughout a lifetime, such that the parental figure is consistently a part of the psyche's process at any stage of development, it reduces the psyche, failing to admit that there is a nuanced change, a proportion to which following its scales of complexification does not offer a composite picture of current reality, but simply a manner of approaching the psyche.

Section Three: Perception and Ideation: The Bridge Between Object and Psyche

There are two ways to ascend toward informational material. One is through the environment, and by that we mean the objects of perception, the things that surround our daily senses, whether through sight, sound, vibration, or sentiment. All of these allow for the appropriation of material that gradually settles into the psyche, enabling the internal process to regulate itself as it sees fit, and through this, the act of thinking occurs.

If one were, for instance, in a desolate area devoid of any trace of human tradition, even a single item can have a longstanding effect. For example, a pen could still appropriate details that bridge back to civilization. Because it is a perceptual item, something available in the environment, it connects to a whole network of data points that reference one another throughout memory. Of course, for someone without the memory of civilization behind them, such a pen would serve little function, but it would still serve some function.

This is why even the slightest contact with an indigenous population can have a profound effect on their thinking. For, though we may not always realize it, within the object itself lie the details that lead back to civilization, not merely as memory, but as something inherent to the perceptual item. It has functionality; it has properties. It presents itself as something manufactured or produced, rather than something that simply belongs to nature. It distinguishes itself from nature as a kind of human abridgment.

In this way, it even exemplifies the human structure, since it manifests the very differentiation the human being has made in relation to themselves. It stands apart from the general function of nature. A tree, by contrast, does not produce such an effect, although, for the reflective mind, it still has an effect, for one recognizes that even within nature there is a process to all things: each specialized in its own way, each true to itself, and not to be conflated with the broader worldly experience of the external world.

There is something consequential in the regular functionality of a tree, which does not define itself by broader or stricter parameters. But because there was never, for the indigenous mind, a sequence of producing an effect of differentiation, this pen that comes before them is immediately in that production. They are forced to secrete themselves from the regular process of worldly attribution or the normal function of experience and instead recognize a differentiation problem, that there is a brain that separates itself from the world in some way.

And so, in and of itself, the perceptual item does imbue that detail beyond its trace of memory, but for the individual, that effect is also produced through memory, because they have had the data references. A pen speaks to the enormous volumes of data imprinted based on the pen, and so on and so forth. That all leads back through memory, but as we have said, it is also based on the object.

Beyond this, however, there is another appropriation of the psyche's functionality that does not rely on the object formation of perception, meaning the pen, for example, whether in its reference or in its ambiguous state and differentiation from regular nature. And that is the ideation that functions on itself.

Now, ideation is not a material object. We cannot build an idea in a literal way because it is another process of the psyche, another construction of it. We cannot literally construct it because it lacks materiality, and while attempts are made to do so, whether through the arts or by articulating the idea in material form, it still does not have the appropriation of material existence.

Yet there is such a thing as ideation, and the ability of the psyche to live upon it and gain vitality through it. This happens because ideation can be seen as the frontal perceptual data of the psyche, almost like the object that serves the psyche as perceptual data. The pen serves the psyche as something of conference; within the psyche itself, there is also the process of structuring its vitality around an idea. The idea stands before the psyche as though external to it, yet not external to the world, somewhere in the middle ground, because the idea is in itself without form or understanding.

This is why certain traditions require that the idea not be questioned, because the idea is meant to serve as this middle ground. It needs a certain formation of materiality, it just is, as it were. Through ideation, one can process the rest of the psyche based in part on that ideation. But one needs to bridge into ideation at times to gain its vitality, because ideation is the bridge between the two worlds. We can thus understand why ideation gives back to the internal world, it serves as the perceptual bridge between worlds.

But ideation also has the ability to connect to perceptual data points. This is why certain ideas are always requisite and others are not, because only those ideas that refer back to a social form of consciousness based on perceptual data, based on the external world, are the ideations that serve that process.

This is why one of the grand ideations based on the external world, one of the grand standings of hominins, is the domestication process, or specifically the familial body. It is an idea fundamentally rather than a perceptual form. It is an idea of family. There is no materiality to that. One might point to the home, but that is merely a reference point to the idea rather than the idea referencing back to the home. The home is not a material function; it serves the idea.

We know this because the second there is a question to relationship or to familial bodies, the home instantly becomes abandoned and useless; the function of its perceptual form cannot transform. It is completely reliant and dependent on the idea. And so, this ideation does lead back to perceptual forms because it is the consequence of the domestication of something grander. Whatever perceptual forms meet that idea, the family body, for example, evolves with public evolution. They are consequential to each other, mutually bound.

That very ideation continues onward to build as the bridge between parts. Therefore, one can function theoretically in the familial space, whether by psyche or by external family bonds, as long as both the ideation reaches back to the public sphere at some intersection, and it functions as a familial internality according to those rules, but most importantly, based on its ideation rather than its perceptual form.

Therefore, one gains no steps in the process of development in the domestic space through anything other than the idea of that domestic space, rather than the space itself. The opposite is true outside of that, where the only method of development is through perceptual data or objects external to the individual, because that is the only habitat of consequence, the one that allows the psyche to function in its proper formation.

Now, saying all that, there exists in the residence of ideation an ability to function with more detail across all processes one seeks to explore. Once one is not reliant on perceptual form, when the perceptual world has little consequence, and ideation is of utmost consequence, one can reach into any perceptual form through the ideation and gain its detail.

The question, then, would be: if that is simply the mode apparatus, can one retract back to regular perceptual forms outside of ideation and then find their function? Because perceptual forms are consequences of one another and dynamically linked, they have little ability to be differentiated and understood in isolation. There is no ability to trace a specific aspect, although one can differentiate through intellect, that intellectuality is itself based on perceptual forms that allowed for differentiation. Thus, one is regulated and controlled by perceptual forms to differentiate perceptual forms. So, is that really differentiation?

But in the case of ideation, if one resides away from those perceptual forms, when one returns to them, one gains access to their full database because one is not reliant on perceptual forms for the vitality of the psyche. Thus, one now gains access to these perceptual forms, though they are themselves based on the ideation. If one does not develop ideation, then the vitality within the perceptual forms lacks substance, they rely on each other.

Moreover, in developing ideation, one must lead it to its consequential end to gain access to perceptual forms, because depth is only allowed as long as there is depth to the ideation, for that is the source of vitality.

So, if one chooses to look at the pen in a domestic space, they require the ideation of that domestic space to reach back into the perceptual form of the pen, leading to its details, details only consequential at that level, because they have suspended reliance on perceptual form. And that is the duo, the difference, between the two sides.

There is an approach to perceptual form that may be advantageous to the overall domestication of its process. This is the socially construed basis for which the definition of the perceptual form is finalized as an afterthought. The idea would be to have a social exemplar insomuch that it provokes sentimentality to its ascendency of contrary suppositions. Differing from Socratic dialogue, which attempts to reduce the subject until its truth is made known; if it is a subject of wealth, we question what it does such a notion owe itself to, and so on. In this case, it is not to reduce a social sentiment but to contrast such, permitting that such is without finding a corroborative perceptual form, to the point where one is compelled to a view from a fairly novel vantage. This process would be extrapolated with diminutive lineage which reaches back to the perceptual form.

For example, the perceptual form may be a 'box', having the sociability of that supposition to include such as a 'container'. Although boxes are not inherently containers, nonetheless we denote a sort of layer of sociability to the object, personifying it as having humanistic characteristics, to which we can then add the addendum of being a 'container'.

However, there remains a lineage to the perceptual form, although requiring an aspect of sociality to finalize the notion of 'container'. The relation from box to container is almost like father to son, distinct but characteristic. Yet, the approach we are mentioning could go a step further, such that in the realm of sociability we could contrast container with box to something that cannot contain, or the notion of containing aspects or things as a recalibration of what was there previously; the point of the matter is to arrive at a said conclusion that may assume a position such as the 'box' for being a 'receptivity form'.

Nevertheless, because the sentiment had arisen through complex social didactic, especially of the contrarian kind, the lineage between the new form and the perceptual form is disrupted. A 'receptivity form' and 'box' do not have a perceptual/social relationship, and it would almost appear metaphysical to approach perceptual forms such as boxes as being feminine, receptacle notions or constructs, since it does not relate to the four-sided object that is before us.

We do retain a sort of intuition that can be applied, much like any other metaphysical theory, yet when attempting to correlate or corroborate there is a fragile lineage to the perceptual basis which remains supreme for the psyche. Thereby, there is a fissure in the perceptual form by virtue of the complexity added to the social process, which has left one ahead in one arena while behind in another. This is analogous to a third cousin relation, which when all is said, is still loosely related, and whatever character is imbued that might offer sentimentality to that relation, would seem unfit as a corroboration by fact of the distance to the relation.

In order to be as transparent as possible, we will demonstrate another example in the effect of these two viewpoints. The perceptual form would be that of a "house"—a structure distinct from a "box" through its reliance on the social construct of the homebody. Nonetheless, we follow this conclusion. When considering its lineage rather than its social interpretation, a house may be defined as a "place of rest." We do not stray far from the perceptual form; rather, we adhere to it, recognizing that its constitution implies a withdrawal from public attention. This progression, from perceptual recognition to social understanding, remains intact and socially coherent.

We can take it a step further, by activating all social possibility, denoting in how a house can become a public sphere, or that the public can be more restful than a house, pushing the boundaries of that social point until we arrive at a conclusion that a house is a privation or domestication of processes. We already would notice the cultish and metaphysical notions of such proclamations, for instance if one were to say, I am returning to my "domesticity," or to my "privation." Yet in the same breath, it would seem much more on cue with the perceptual form if one were to say, "I am going to rest from this," or generally, "I need to go home and rest."

The lineage between perceptual form and 'rest' is forthcoming and fills the language of normal sociability, which social development through contrast and deliberation has removed from the perceptual form but does offer the advantage of a more accurate portrayal of the perceptual form. The truth of a house is domesticity, but because the perceptual form does not imbue in as much, and we only arrive at that conclusion through social 'tricks', we lose that lineage.

If there is a perceptual form that does have a direct lineage to say, privation, then we can apply it back into the perceptual form and utilize it within regular social bearings. For instance, the use of the notion of 'privacy concerns' which is centered on the perceptual form of a state-like, or corporeal system, which are perceptual forms that overextend to all matters of life, thereby with little deviation to apply a social sentiment to construe the notion of 'privacy'. Note that it functions as a noun, most would not say they are entering into their privacy arena, but rather refer to it by its state-like system, emphasizing its effects and the sentiments, often adverse, that accompany it.

As well, the perceptual form of acts of violence which occur in home-like settings would be called domestic violence. Although there is no matter in the violence itself of being 'domestic', we take the perceptual form of 'home-like' and 'violence' to then apply certain social congruency with the term domestic violence. This does not deviate from the perceptual lineage, despite the fact that the only manner to understand the notion of domestic aspects is through a complex approach to the notion of home.

Yet, paradoxically, we cannot term the house as a domesticity, at least in regular sociability, but we rely upon it to offer the term for violence that occurs within its domain. The reason is that we cannot follow the strict perceptual form and dictate that what is occurring is house violence, since it limits all forms of violence which occur based on a family body, whether within the house or not. We cannot even use the term familial violence since there are forms of familial attachment or sequence that are not strictly family-based.

We are compelled into a corner until the only probable term that would include all that we require of the experience would be domestic violence. However, the arrival to the term has not been through a social course at formulating all that is possible from a perceptual form, but only that the judicial proceeding cannot approach it in any other way without bearing ambiguous terminology. The term does not attempt and has not arisen based on an understanding of domesticity, but rather that there is no other term which works.

We can even go a step further and say that there is no perceptual form that has a direct lineage to domestic violence, despite its compelled conclusion, and therefore it is not an applicable term for general social use, but rather for institutional proceedings. This does not mean that there is no reality to domestic violence, but rather that there is no direct lineage to its perceptual form, which, if we were to follow many other judicial notions, would bear similar conclusions.

Section Five: Perceptual Forms and the Institutionalization of Depression

The Northern Hemisphere has higher rates of depression, explained by various factors, especially = sunlight exposure (Smith, 2018).iii In addition to the exploration of the psychological manifestation of depression, one can surely notice that once we discuss the level of sunlight exposure, we are beginning to formulate an opinion regarding the entire scope of the depressive state. If such environmental factors have causative power, then we must attribute some or most of the depressive state to an environmental phenomenon and not a psychological one. Although the study does discuss biological correlations, such as vitamin D deficiency, we can explain the process from the perceptual modality, where we face a philosophical quandary if biological happenstance precedes or succeeds brain processes in a chosen activity in addition to environmental aspects. (Anglin, 2013).iv

Although sunlight is a correlation, it is more so the isolated environment or the structural separation that creates the possibility to embody that sensibility within one's subjective state, meaning to say, it is an architectural manifestation of individuality: the individual expresses themselves through the modality of that isolation, such that it is an institutionalized awareness of structural reality.

We become discomfited when we begin the journey to identify every single factor of the environment which produces psychological symptoms, which, in effect, only dictates the causation itself is not psychological but rather perceptual. The outcome is usually to account for the environmental factors, but that would be handed to the stoic counselor who then dictates life choices, or the architect or city planner, as such a list reaches into many disciplines. But to remain in the field of psychology, the progressive question shall be: in what ways have perceptual forms been internalized to the point of embodiment, all against the backdrop of one's regular psychological state. (Modzelewski, 2025).v

In the case of depression, the embodiment of the perceptual form is such that the individual is comfortable in a structure situated without constant interaction with the public, not comfortable in the sense of a deficiency of abuse. When we define comfort as a structural stagnation from outside disruptions, then we find a possible embodiment of that state, which does not perform with the regular social fluidity of the outside world, but only in the way a 'comfortable' space would interact ambiently in isolation.

Almost as a form of abandonment, which again is not personal abandonment (which, of course, can be amplified by attachment to the perceptual form), but rather that the structure itself is experiencing abandonment, or is shallow as would be depicted in a horror scenario. In such a scenario, the individual who should detach from the place remains attached and thereby embodies such an existence. It might not even be psychological at all, but rather the embodiment of that perceptual experience, meaning that it is almost impossible for certain systems to contain depression, even while other psychological symptoms are possible.

We are asserting that the underlying thought patterns that give rise to depression are a psychological aspect and thus referred to by Freud quite strictly as melancholy, and not depression (Freud, 1917). Because in the general sense, melancholy can be romantic, or at least not depressive, as understood in the contemporary era (Freud, 1917; Parker). vi,vii

Rather, the depressive aspect is whereby one depresses themselves to the point of experienced isolation based on a perceptual form. Even the notion of depression requires a third-party element, someone or something must be performing the depressing process, and in the case of other psychological symptoms such as anxiety, the term is derived from its manifestation. We could almost imagine a 'Western' clinically depressed person participating in a remote village and losing the depressive aspect of their melancholic thought patterns, unless, that is, they recreate their structural environment within that space, such that they embody that sensibility with a certain imaginative stretch.

All psychological symptoms can participate in or partially embody a perceptual form. For instance, anxiety manifests through the mechanical dysfunction found in its own process; bipolar disorder reflects nature's contradictions; and compulsion exhibits a stern consistency found in nature. What differs from depression is that the foremost aspect relates to the perceptual form, whereas anxiety (and other conditions) do not fully perpetuate such formation. There is little found in the structural reality which correlates with bipolar disorder, perhaps in how the house contradicts the street, or how the street contradicts the sidewalk. A bipolar individual is not necessarily embodying that disparity to the same effect that we can find a correlation between sunlight and depression. Still, there is some level of perceptual form which, first, perpetuates the psychological experience (which without, would lose validity in the internal system), and second, amplifies that very psychological premise. The commencement of the symptom is psychological, but there are various perceptual forms that animate its vitality, although removing them is different from what is advocated by those suggesting simply changing the perceptual from (e.g., researchers promoting more sunlight) (Smith, 2018).viii

In the case of anxiety, at most, the tension is found in other beings. One who interacts with highly tense individuals will not experience the interaction based on a perceptual form: first, because sociality is familiar and thus part of a domesticating process (a relation, rather than a perceptual formation); and second, because any tension in a populace is contrasted with structural reality, which does not sustain that tension. Mechanical creations, e.g., traffic, are a contemporary difficulty because they, in fact, offer a perceptual form of heightened tension. Industry and the mechanical outsourcing of human processes do offer the greatest perceptual form of tension, other than that of beings themselves. In the mechanical case, we cannot dismiss its perceptual form and, thus, noticing their internal tension, whether in producing their objective or in internal-external tension, where they are a utility to the human process despite participating in human individuality: much in the way a subservient being manifests natural tension by way of their loss of autonomy, all the while serving a utility for what is above them. (Arendt, 1958).ix

Their individuality is pronounced to such a degree that the tension is noticed in the environment. Yet in the mechanical case, it is not social but rather structural, so that there is no process of sociality that undermines the perceptual experience like that of a servant (e.g., shared household processes), and therefore meets the social eye with all its tension intact. The reason that physical structures do not behold such tension, even as they are secluded from the general environment, is because they have openings, in and out, that continue structurally, despite social precautions, which are not perceptual. However, a structure without windows, doors, or any openings will, in fact, be experienced as a perceptual tension.

Even the terminology exemplifies this: the social term in the application of other symptoms is not found, such as clinical anxiety or clinical schizophrenia, but we proclaim the notion of clinical depression because there is an institutionalized element to depression in its fundamental state: that it is institutionalized as a perceptual experience rather than a psychological one, at least in the form it takes during the depressive experience. Hippocrates, for instance, described melancholy as a derivative of something otherworldly and thus a disease rather than a psychological manifestation (Hippocrates, ca. 400 BCE; Panksepp, 2011)x,xi

As van Praag (1993) notes, the "biology" uncovered in mental disorders appears "to be devoid of diagnostic specificity," adding, "pseudo-entities. it would be little less than a miracle if . a single marker . would be found identifying such an 'entity.'" Although the neuro-psycheality of psychological symptoms has helped the argument by serving a psychological premise (we have cerebral data to prove it), since perceptual forms and all of the environment are producers of our physiology, it does not move the argument forward (Panksepp, 2011).xii, xiii

Van Praag (1993) might not continue the argument by dictating the perceptual form to which there is an embodiment, and is a far stretch to call them pseudo-entities, being that they are found in the external world, are perceptually activated, and may be a way of saying that it is outside the realm of psychology and rather on account of the environment with which the individual intersects in an improbable manner.

Moreover, depression requires participation in a certain structural realm to manifest. This also explains why there is more perpetuation in the psychological field to prove depression as a psychological aspect rather than a perceptual form, because then it departs from psychology and moves toward the stoic life choices tied to structural environments.

First, we can alleviate the researchers' fears if we admit the final stage of depression, which of the depressive aspect of melancholy, is an experience embodied by the perceptual environment, especially the structural organization. Yet, we do so not because stoic life choices are its first pedigree. Instead, we can offer the remedy of recognizing that there is remains a psychological state that decides to embody a perceptual form to the degree for which an individual finds no other favor than continuity in that perceptual loop, such that they avoid sunlight as opposed to merely being in a habitat with a lack of sunlight. They recreate the structural environment to mirror the very embodiment of that structural environment.

This is where the study of depression continues in the psychological department, such that it would be best to study the individual who attaches to the perceptual form, rather than underline the understanding of what it takes to embody the perceptual form, which, if we remain in the psychological department, would offer little benefit to either the researcher or the patient. For the patient is not being offered the avenue of stoic life choices since they are in the habitat of psychological analysis. Still more so, we are offering the recognition of that very reality and validating the institutionalized nature, but more so validating the perceptual form to which the patient is bound in that loop, such that by calling it clinical depression we have asserted that the patient is correct in assuming that the embodiment of a perceptual form is a proper psychological process, and should remain in said position.

This analysis is not to conclude that there is no validity to the depressive state, only that most of its aspects remain in non-psychological domains, and thereby should either be alleviated through those departments, counseling, stoic life choices, environmental choices, basically anything related to individual interactivity with the external environment, or can be premised on how one continues to participate in a perceptual form to the extent of embodiment, which is based on a psychological makeup.

In the case of anxiety, one may choose to follow external processes that interact with perception, such as engaging with the mechanical formations of human activity, including technology, or to trace the emergence of internal anxiety, which may appear similar on the surface but follows a subconscious progression that can, in fact, be outlined through analysis. In the case of a perceptual form, there is no subconscious background to such a form. No level of analysis of the individual (although the structural realm would be a different story) would reach a nuanced level of subconscious material in that experience.

The only method to continue the psychological process and find a subconscious lineage is through the initial choice of partaking in that realm, which is somewhat arbitrary as well, for the material based on a single choice is not very large, and thus would be exploring a very diminutive aspect of one's psyche. We could, in theory, underline the subconscious lineage of the reaction to that environment; however, that is merely the reaction to the current setting, to which the entire problem remains. Such an analysis might be beneficial after the fact, to where one explores the psychological makeup of their reaction to a perceptual form, which also might not be substantial in consideration of one's entire makeup.

The one area of the psyche that is both psychologically substantial and would assist in the current perceptual form is the general criteria for attaching oneself to perceptual forms, which might be uncovered as dependency on environment or other substantiated aspects. (Oldenburg, 1989)xiv

One can gain access to a perceptual form via a perceptual experience itself or through preliminary domesticated content. In the case of the former, one partially enters into a sphere that contains unexpected inferences. For the expected inferences, such as regular daily activity, these are already considered a preliminary domesticated setting because of the developed internal experiences based on that expectation. The unexpected influence, which does not entail a preliminary picture, would be considered a direct perceptual experience. Surely, there are elements that will have preliminary domesticated backings, but the aspects that are offered through unexpected inferences make for a direct perceptual form.

For example, a conversation with a friend to which there was no preliminary development, besides the backdrop of the friendship, would entail some unexpected inferences that would be considered direct perceptual forms. However, whatever those unexpected perceptual inferences are, they will be laid upon the psyche to have later dissemination in accordance with selfhood. During the interaction with a direct perceptual form, one has enabled a disruption against their selfhood to make an allowance for their sentience of that unexpected perceptual form. Because of this, it is only a utility for later dissemination, for at the moment of experience one has no direct connection other than the impact itself. (Brooks, 2025)xv

This is the preliminary subtext of what has come to be known as survivor's guilt, which is the direct perceptual form based on an unexpected circumstance. It then causes one to reflect back upon themselves, to question their validity of existence in reference to that perceptual experience. It would seem that if it were based on an experience that was a direct perceptual form wherein there was preliminary domesticated content, one would assent to that perceptual form based on that preliminary data, such that one would not reflect back upon the perceptual form itself for dissemination, but rather on how that domesticated content interacted with the perceptual form. (Freud, 1917)xvi

Direct perceptual information is thus a retractable notion and has the coinciding religious constitution of redemption or retribution, which is the setting ground toward reversing the very interaction of the perceptual information to include aspects of personhood and thus construct domesticated content. What benefits this process is the authentic aspect that serves a direct perceptual formation, so that one becomes enfranchised with a sort of reality that is lost from purview when there is preliminary or expected infrastructure toward a perceptual form. However, what it lacks is a modality of personhood that takes precedence over the perceptual form, such that one may enact a disruptive form of behavior that truly is not an emanation of selfhood, but rather how they embody the perceptual form. (Arendt, 1958)

The mistaken conjecture of redemption is that there existed a true failure in the rapture of that perceptual modality, which, of all things, is not part of personhood. It can reflect the choice beforehand, the failure of preliminary investigation, or the lack of reflection after the occurrence, but the direct failure itself is most distant from personhood and is quite arbitrary when taken too seriously. We can very well measure the reverse of redemption, that of a taxing, domesticated setup such as daily routine, which can also be assumed to lack participation with perceptual information and thus be detrimental to the psyche process. Without the perceptual form incorporated, the domesticated modality will follow a deviating precedent based on an internality that has no basis in reality, which eventually will have its time of day and reveal its flaws. Both processes are to be found as flawed, only having direct perceptual experience as part of their composition and integral to their final outcome.

One may be in awe at the very act of such behavior, such that it would seem they have a corrupted psyche through which such actions take place when put under pressure. But in fact, it is the opposite of the matter, where a true embodiment takes place in the perceptual form, which utilizes personhood as its host to express its data stream. It is akin to one participating in a prison environment with an elevated level of criminality. It will eventually culminate in serving as a context for themselves or in embodying that infrastructure against the premonitions of personhood. It is truly not they who are interacting, and the aspect of choice was only in assenting to that environment. But once contained by that environment and interacting with direct perceptual form, all is already completed in terms of personhood, and it is only now that they express the formality of that perceptual form.

This does shed light on the developing science of behavior as a reference point for the psychological state of an individual. While serving the most immediate results, being that behavior is most attached to a social reality of perceptual forms, it lacks the very connection to personhood itself. It is possibly the least psychological aspect of the psyche, as behavior is most expressive of perceptual forms that do not adjoin with the psyche's buildup. Instead, behavior is most attributed to the process of externality, which surely could alleviate symptoms when change occurs in the perceptual realm, but is a far stretch in dealing with the individual psychological makeup.

If short-term symptom alleviation is one's objective, then look no further than behavior and general regulation of externalities. However, if long-term comprehension of one's psychological makeup is the objective, then behavior study is the least formatted for that process. Such a science would be better suited to the direct study of infrastructure and its expressions that make their way into behavioral patterns, but more so to granting the research all its ramifications rather than merely symptom-related aspects.

The argument may be that behavior is, in fact, the emanation of psychological makeup. Yet such a claim is inconclusive, since behavior is related to real-time interaction with the social realm, not the psychological. Behavior is based on instant choice-activity, which is completely vulnerable to perceptual forms and general externalities. Psychological choices that are not part of that choice-social-activity are surely a great study for psychology, but once we enter the sphere of perceptual form, we are bound to the expressive embodiment of all externalities, to which an individual is almost insignificant as part of the system. (Foucault, 1977)

This is why shadow environments can disrupt the psyche: one may embody the expression of those perceptual forms to the point of acting upon the shadow more than any other aspect of personhood seeking expression. The shadow differs from other localities because it is fundamentally a perceptual form flawed by its composition, such that embodying and experiencing that aspect will corrupt the psychological makeup of an individual.

We can further the premise of the archetype of Jung, which was a modeled explanation for the communal presence in an individual and found at the deep ends of their psychological presence, which can have some alleviation from its psychological premise and rather be explained in how the individual embodies a perceptual form that constitutes itself as an archetype. (Jung, 1968)xvii

Archetypes are not an embedded feature of an individual's psychological makeup or based on how it references itself in contrast to the community, but rather, more simply, the expressive formation of an individual that loses their individuality in reference to a perceptual form. This is why all the archetypes have universal themes that can be found in the construction of the universe, such as birth, utility, order, disruption, all of which can be traced to antiquated Theos, such as found within the Egyptian dynasty. The reason is fairly simple: because these universal themes can be found as perceptual forms in the universe, they will be imbued with an expressive formation comprising the individual so long as there is direct interaction with the perceptual form.

If one bears the perceptual form of a birthing experience in regards to any element in nature, whether it is a tree or the birthing of a familiar human, such a perceptual form and its expressive format is the archetype. Although given attributes based on associative religions, it is the same construct. It is not, as Jung postulated, the expressive formation of psychological makeup. In fact, it is a direct deviation from psychology and is rather the process of uncovering external reality, to which there is a mistaken notion of an individual expressing that very reality.

It is with some irony that we arrive at this conclusion because it is noted that most major religions have their archetypal figures. If we follow the leader's subjective psychology, we would not find that archetype, for they must present themselves from a former archetype. So the conclusion is rather not a psychological expression but a perceptual form that happens to coincide with an individual who had a momentary lapse into that expression without any individualized interaction.

It is rather a weakness that one is archetypical, and in a regular social format, if one is assessed as archetypical, they would be viewed with a negative attribute, as they have not formed their psychological makeup but have rather constituted themselves in the expression of the perceptual form.

The problem with studying the psychological makeup of an individual is that we inevitably encounter the intersection between the individual, society, and external influences. This is why it has become prevalent to associate psychology with personality types, despite the fact that a personality type, by its very nature, is an externality, not a generality of individual makeup.

One's personality is very much a part of the external forms through which they express themselves, and their psychological happenstance is made up of various movements despite the prevalence of those perceptual forms. For example, one of the five personality types is constituted as being orderly, which is very much the expressive form of the perceptual experience of an orderly system, to which they express that form within themselves. When we find orderliness as their modality, it is not an expression of their psychological makeup, but rather in how their psychological makeup interacts with the perceptual form that happens to be constituted as being orderly.

Although we commonly associate a personality type to be a lifelong format, if one changes their perceptual form in a dramatic manner, or develops their psychological happenstance separate from their perceptual form, it is very much the case that one could become a different personality based on that very factor.

A general premise is that anything that could be found in an antiquated Theos of yesteryear would be constituted as a perceptual formation, for there are thousands of years of history to maintain the same universal elements. Such that it has little to do with an individual, but rather with the manner in which they coincide with the universe. Such that the Egyptian Theos of order is common for Egyptian dynasties, and with Mesopotamia and others, because of its universal form.

To then say that such a personality type is the psychological makeup of an individual is to say that the individual is simply an expressive aspect of perceptual forms. Although it is one aspect of how individuals process the psyche, or how the psyche processes itself, it is by its very definition not individualistic. It is no different when a tree and bush grow alongside in an orderly fashion than when an individual has found themselves to be orderly. We are not discussing individuals anymore, but rather nature.

This would be the same for zodiac signs, which are universal elements of nature and perceptual forms for an individual, but in no way are they distinguished to an individual. Rather, they are separated by the arbitrary nature of how one interacts with the universe, not in the sense of interaction, but rather in the way they embody the universe, with no individualistic sense. If we want to study the individual makeup itself, then we enter the course of psychology, rather than utilizing the individual to study the universe.

Section Seven: The Limits of Perception and the Invention of Narrative Correlation

There are two modalities of perception or perceptual form which do not inherently connect. One sees an object before them, separates from, and then views another object. Those two objects have no relationship and, as such, remain according to the psyche as distinct entities of certain significance. Because of this problem, that of relationality between perceptual forms, one applies a variety of methods to adjoin those two perceptual forms, or rather in some cases, to deal with it in a manner that does not have that disparity equate a disruption for the psyche.

The simplest of processes for two distinct perceptual forms is to create an arbitrary addendum that dictates a correlation between those two entities, despite the fact that there is no perceptual form that agrees with that supposition, for they are distinct and will always remain distinct. Rather, there will be an arbitrary creation of the psyche that correlates to them, not so much from any perceptual data, but rather as a re-imagination of an arbitrary array of perceptual data that could be postulated as the intermediary between those two perceptual forms.

The composite of this intermediary articulation is made up of correlating factors of each of those objects of perception. Therefore, it would be natural that the intermediary factor has already been in the process of interpretation for the perceptual form so that it can conclude a substantiation for both sides; to formulate a correlated composite picture.

For instance, if one sees a bed and then sees a car as the next perceptual form, with disparity between them, then the correlating factor can be sleeping and transit, as well as something that adjoins those two elements. For instance, transitional phases of regular activity to which both correlate. As of now, one has been able to proceed in the correlation between these two perceptual forms and thus allowed the psyche to be in a linear process, instead of dealing with the disparity of those distinct perceptions.

When one postulates an intermediary correlation, there must be a justification for the imprint. In our case, the correlating factor of transitional phases must be, in itself, something that relates to a third perceptual form. One has no ability to ascend the notion of transitional phases unless they have a further correlation; in what way that proceeds to be a part of the psyche. For our example, it becomes abundantly clear that transitional phases is the notion of a linear process of life to which there are regular phases and transitional phases. More so, there is the correlating factor that one concerns themselves with: the separation between regular and transitional.

Thereby, an aspect of the correlating factor is a narrative conjunction that precludes the perceptual forms to conclude a composite picture, in this case, of a life process to which one is participating. It is linear because of the very fact that two dots on the plane are in a correlating system, with the existential experience substantiates a reason that they require correlation.

Correlation is unjust to its regular definition because it simply demonstrates how one aspect is in relationship to another. However, there is always a third aspect to which one is correlating, and how something correlates- correlates. This is not a philosophical undercut but rather the primal supposition of correlation. We would not utilize the word correlation unless we are attempting to connect two aspects in accordance with a third aspect. If not, we would consider using the word adjoin or attach, which is better suited to how a screw fastens to a plank of wood. We would not dictate that a screw correlates to a plank of wood all because it fastens to it. It is only a matter of correlation when there is an observer that relates to the correlation.

Therefore, when we correlate the bed with the car, we are not only adjoining those two aspects based on material that is found within each of them, it is rather the case that we are concerned with how we relate to that very correlating aspect. We will term the aspect that correlates to the correlation as the third factor.

The third factor is the attempt to propose a framework upon reality that is above and beyond one's realized reality. This is the close parallel with narrative structures, which utilize the same process; by moving beyond the screw and plank of wood, one requires some theoretical system that does not bind itself with screws and bolts. The instant we enter that sphere, it can be considered somewhat metaphysical. So that when one interacts with the third factor of our case, that of transitional phases, it is really the general theory of the process of time and cyclical systems, which is abstract and theoretical to the experienced state of physicality.

The quintessential cycle is that of day and night. To view it as a cyclical format rather than an experienced reality is to say that there is somehow a relationship between day and night, or more importantly, that there is somehow a third factor in regard to day and night that positions each of those aspects as if they are connected to the other. It would be metaphysical to claim that somehow the night interacts with the day or vice versa, for they are differing aspects. If they truly interact, then they are part of the same physical structure and therefore not distinct entities. Either we say that they are distinct entities, to which we require a metaphysical claim upon their correlation, or we conclude that the day is simply the night in the general universe system, so that they are not distinct at all and therefore do not have the ability to form any cycle.

A correlating factor is a single modality adjoining two distinct perceptual forms, which so happens to be a narrative structure. The narrative aspect is technically that which does not deserve to adjoin, but is given the right of passage through the narrative work. As Katie Queseda notes, there is no narrative without conflict, to which we will add the supplementary note that it is not the structure of a narrative to have conflict, but rather the only manner to position a narrative being in the case where there is conflict.xviii

From the conflicting vantage, one requires a narrative structure to correlate the two opposing aspects: the one before the conflict, and the one proceeding the conflict. In the case where there is no conflict, it is a perfected form of experience to which there is no need for narrative. One enjoys a narrative structure more so than any other form of communication because they are embedded in a life experience filled with conflict, through which they find validation, alleviation, and justification for their subjective experiences of that very conflict. More so, they find semblance to the very topic of our discussion, to which they have more ability in dealing with the disparity between perceptual forms via the narrative structure. Thus it is not simply the experience of the story, but rather the conceptual format embedded within the story that is required; to amend two perceptual forms.

This also explains the disparity between narratives in stories, which both serve as a primordial system and a powerful force for social communication. It is not considered archaic, as evidenced by the strong scientific research on narrative's role in human development. Nor is it seen as the overarching theme of society, in the way a primordial family might be situated.xix

If such is the case, we have explained the very conundrum by the fact that the narrative is in itself a remedy for conflict. As well, a mature psyche would not require the constant comprehension and application of conflict, or the process of correlating two perceptual forms or correlating two sides of a conflict, for they have subjectively understood the process. As two children that are fighting might be told to 'grow up', for maturity leaves the need of most conflict. Thereby, narrative structures are both powerful in the resolution of conflict and vulnerable in their proposition of themselves as a formidable system of life, when in fact, they are simply the remedy to a problem.

The reason that a narrative does in fact provide a resolution to conflict is that we estimate a correlation between the two sides of the conflict, which in a regular case would not adjoin. The hero finds themselves at odds with an expectation. The conflict is apparent: the hero in contrast to the expectation. We seem to forget that the resolution, in which the hero fulfills that expectation or one similar to it, is not an adjoining of a prior conflict. Rather, another track is overlaid on the prior one. Where failure was before, success is now, yet they do not intermingle. The narrative structure compels one to view them in succession because it seeks to adjoin what is regularly impossible to adjoin.

Therefore, every narrative has a value statement, which can be viewed as the justification found in the metaphysical realm of morality or value, through which these two parts can, in fact, connect. Redemption is a metaphysical trait since the physical realm only accepts the current process in real-time. This is why narrative and religion are so closely related, as they utilize the same conceptual map: that of something metaphysical to explain material reality. In the case of a narrative structure, it is to justify and amend conflict. In the case of religion, it is to provide an entire metaphysical framework to relate to reality.

If we notice, a narrative structure does not concern the value as much as the conflict. Although in some cases the value or the justification for conflict can be a very elaborate scheme, the objective of the narrative is to resolve conflict with a metaphysical justification. One can elicit a story or narrative structure in order to imbue a set of principles or values, but that is the proposition of conflict in order to teach a lesson. Comparable to the creation of disparity between parent and child only so the child will require a redemption from that conflict. The objective of the narrative is to face and find resolution, as most would admit the climax is the purpose of the story, not the value embedded within its structure. When a person senses that a proposed story is formatting for the value more so than the resolution to its innate vulnerability, they reserve themselves from interacting as though there is something disconcerting with that process.

A narrative structure conceals its value attribution in order to be considered a socially adaptable story. Its most dramatic exemplification is its conflict, and resolution is already found in the sequence of having a proposition of a narrative. We find stories that do not resolve the conflict are still resolute, considering that they are immersed in a conflict, where the viewer has performed the resolution by participating in both sides, making for a coherent setting. The justification for the conflict, or the value statement, is concerned with the viewer in regard to the conflict.

Therefore, the perspective of a narrative arc is not comprehensive enough, since all that is required is a linear sequence with an embedded conflict. The notion that it must angle corresponding to an arc may not be required, since leading and proceeding from the conflict can be without change or internal resolution. When the viewer resolves the conflict by agreeing to the sequence, they are not the climactic element of the proverbial arc but utilize the dramatic imprint of the conflict to relate to the infraction of the sequence. If we follow the value attribution, we will notice that in the event of no resolution, as no change is inherent, such as the most extreme tragedy where only the perpetual continuation of its sequence takes place, the justification for the conflict is the viewer or observer.

When we follow the pattern of an unarticulated story, such as a direct statement of occurrence, the observer is found to be the only aspect of the resolution by virtue of listening. The justification for the unarticulated conflict is not received by the act of listening, such that the resolution is merely the presence or validation of listening. The resolution is to bear witness to the actuality of the story rather than the embedded resolution based on the statement. Because the conflict was not articulated, there is no reason for the narrative function, more so for a resolution to that conflict. The only pillar that a narrative statement relies upon is the observer or listener, and in the absence of that, it would lose all correlation to a narrative structure. If one follows an internal proposition of a narrative statement, such as "I went to school," it would not bear a consistency to a narrative function. However, the moment it is externalized, the listener allows such to be a narrative, both by a presumed supplement of information, for there must be more that is included in the overall experience of that statement; and by the observational resolution to the fact that 'they went to school.' By witnessing and providing social validation to the story, they are inadvertently participating in the ongoing story by exemplifying that it is true. The conflict, in this case is the lack of social validation, and the resolution is that there is now a recognition of such.

There is a regulatory prospect that is administered to the notion of purporting a domesticated process, whereas it must negotiate in all its procedures that it will, in effect, return to the perceptual realm. Whenever there is deviation from the perceptual realm, accompanying that deviation is the perceptual process that allows and succeeds in continuing and abating by that deviation. We cannot consider that the perceptual realm is completely denigrated of its task, so that now a deviation is merely a novel process of the psyche, only that the perceptual realm begins to service that deviation while perpetually moving between its internal requirement of continuance and the deviating process.

The way it handles this dichotomy is through a cycle, in which it begins with the perceptual aspect, with the deviating factor (say, a domesticated process) disrupting the continuance, and then succeeding in following its own construct. At no point in the deviation is there a loss of the chain of custody back to the perceptual object; only that it has damaged the initial imprint, whereas now it follows its own set of rules, while utilizing that imprint at every turn to continue its stimulation. This cycle can occur fairly quickly, which has one enter back into the perceptual realm to begin the process again.

The psyche is transgressing the perceptual object or imprint so that it can follow a deviating pattern, but its remnants remain in the deviating pattern to further stimulate its process. There is no animation without perceptual imprints, and when we remove the possibility of perceptual access, without access to the senses or to a change in external forms, whatever ability of the body to participate with the external realm will be the forerunner of the deviating pattern, which is compelled to the forefront. When the perceptual realm is not forthcoming (for instance, a secluded room for an extended period), the psyche is incentivized to deviate, for in each attempt at perceptual access, it is met with similarity. The nemesis of perceptual objects is similarity, for it assumes that the current realm is based on the initial imprints, so that what is being seen after an extended period of exposure is merely the formation of memory. Similarity invokes the notion of memory, which is a deviating pattern from the perceptual realm by definition of its bygone associations.

We can view this process as a form of borrowing, where the lender is the perceptual form, and the subsequent event is receiving the loan, to distribute away from the direction of the lender, but ultimately is connected and reverted to the lender, that of the perceptual form. The return is based on that chain of custody, so that not only is there an allowance set for the deviated factor to distribute up to a certain degree, but that degree is defined by how deviated that factor is. For when the deviation is most dissimilar from the perceptual imprint (or the lender), it retrieves the animation most quickly. The other side of the spectrum has that which is most similar to the initial imprint, such that it would not be considered a deviating factor of a dramatic degree, and because of this, it would be animated for quite a bit longer. It follows the chain of custody so that it retains continuance de facto of its realization of the imprint despite deviation.

For example, to follow the case in point, if a friend or a family member is the lender, and there is familial continuation in how the process of loan distribution works based on that familiarity, the collection of that loan will be most extended, or even forgiven to some degree. While in the case of a lender most unfamiliar with the borrower, or in the case where they do not follow a succession from initial contractual sentiment, the case would be that collection is most approximate. Forgiveness of loans is usually associated with a familial attachment or continuity, while overbearing loan terms occurs when there are non-familial aspects that create disparity between lender and borrower.

The lender is most agreeable to have their money and subjective association of their persona participate in the distribution process, such that they would gain a sensibility that the loan had never really left their hands, being distributed as much the same as their sentiment of the subject. When there is a sense of a distribution network that creates a dissociation with the persona of the lender, they will find themselves in a place of collection, to recollect what is missing of their subjective associations, which now seems lost.

In fact, if we study the subject adequately, we realize that all lending is never in regards to money and its associated power, but rather with the connection to the distribution process. This is why familial institutions or tight-knit communities are able to retain and proliferate their wealth, as the lending process is free of the constraints of disparity, since the distribution retains that familiarity throughout the process, such that no one would be considered lenders or borrowers, but rather participants in an organization of distribution.

Section Ten: Perceptual Modality and the Dynamics of Reality

Distinguishing perceptual modality is a process in which, instead of proceeding as an interactive realm based on a separation of a sequence (like a gated sphere), it is the attention sphere of perceptual information that is focused and deliberate, thereby not precluding the broader backdrop but rather facilitating its own merits as if it were broader reality.

For the psyche itself, there is no distinction, as perceptual information is its first impression of all possible reality, such that it is not a differentiation but rather a perceptual modality. The reason being that there is no ability to perceive everything, and one must account for certain parameters of perception as a finite institution for the broader initiation of perceptual reality. When one views the world as the real world, they are simply following a criterion of perception, which has issued a declaration of being a specimen of the entire world or all of reality. There is no hamper within the psyche to differentiate its parameters from broader reality, and in some sense, the gates are opened, or, to be more particular, there are no gates, only a periphery of attention, and whatever eventual changes occur, there is no contention or issue on the psyche's part, for it would follow whichever way it proceeds to go.

If there is a claim of impartiality, it is not upon the individual but only an environmental differentiation, to which this so happens to be a margin of perceptual information that does not include enough information to be measured as a core value to presume an orientation to "reality."

For example, within the marginalized locations of a civilization or state, whatever the perceptual information, it would be impartial by the very fact that the entire structural reserve is marginalized to a point where, in the inclusion of the entire spectrum of that specific locality, it would merely be a symbolic measure of a certain reflection of the central localities, such that the environment can be considered inherently biased by its own constitution.

However, in this particular example, the perceptual modality would not assist in acclimating to the partiality of that encapsulation, and only another mechanism of the psyche can assert the supposition that the entire entity is marginalized, and whatever the perceptual information, it would be inherently lacking form as being an impartial evidence of reality.

More so, it supposes itself as a perceptual point of inflection when, in fact, its entire construction and constitution are based on another perceptual point. Even as there is a seeming real entity called this marginalized entity, in service to perception, it does not exist, and any postulation that it does will only cause the psyche to presume a reality function when, in fact, there is not. Worse still, it would have the true nature of reality as a circumvention since there is a generated conflict between these two perceptual modalities.

This results in a weary supposition for our inquiry, in which it is being postulated that known reality, brick and stone, roads, houses, can all be considered non-perceptual, which is a claim that seems exacting. However, we can follow our internal logic to where, if we enter an indigenous locality or a desert for that matter, although seeming to contain perceptual information, all would agree in such experience that the perceptual experience is not conclusive, despite finding brick and stone, roads, and houses. It is merely a matter of perspective and scale in accordance with regular living that has one find such a supposition to be exacting and inconclusive.

Perceptual modality differs from an interactive domain, which from the outset separates itself in order to participate more wholeheartedly in its interactive elements. But in this way, it is simply the attention toward a specific modality of perception without the intent of serving as a demarcation of broader perceptual information. It is in the realm of attention that this will manifest in either the interactive or distinguished perceptual modality. If it is simply the encapsulation of a perceptual parameter without the attempted differentiation, then it is the latter; if it is to separate as distinguished, then it is the former.

It would seem like an impossible feat, for one would require the direction of parameters of attention so that it is a perceptual modality while all being undifferentiated from the broader perceptual domain. For if, in the event that one enters into that sphere with any intention of maintaining a specific perceptual modality, it is the case that one enters into an interactive domain but without the attributes of complete interactivity, since they are still attempting to experience perceptual reality as it were; delineating their internal process of interpretation that is interactive. This very mistake is the occurrence of domesticating perceptual reality, for which they maintain perceptual modality but with strict parameters disallowing information outside that modality, but not so much as to differentiate that domain as different from general perceptual reality, thereby having them acclimate to a true perceptual domain but with some interactiveness that causes them to domesticate reality.

The opposite end of the spectrum would have one follow perceptual modality but without nuance to the experience of attention, such that it is not the setting of parameters as a psyche process (for that is the case of differentiation), but rather where one follows the attention of specific perceptual experience to an acclimated depth, such that with the dial upon depth of attention toward perception, one regulates the perceptual modality. But in the experience of the object, whatever the object of perception is, it is by no choice of the perceptual modality but merely the initial decision of depth of attention that is the only process by which one obtains and retains a certain modality of perception.

The case of trauma, for instance, would be a compelled version of a high degree of attention toward perceptual objects. In such a case, one obtains a modality of perception that encapsulates a strong degree of a version of reality. This is only distinguished from regular reality by its nuanced perspective of reality, yet it would be considered a true form of reality in all contexts. This is because there was no psyche process applied to that perceptual information, merely the regulation of uncontrolled perceptual depth.

We notice the objective similarity in the narratives of traumatic experiences across an era or period of time. It is always the case that there exists a true encapsulation of perceptual reality. The only difference lies in the fact that the point of distinction merely assesses the same direction toward perceptual information as it was in that period of time.

When perception is extrapolated in a desynchronized manner, the cause of which will be an encapsulation of its premise as if it were obtainable and tenable. There are two modalities to desynchronizing perceptual data: one is the disruption of its infrastructural nature, such as a barrier, or the applicable personal realm layered upon the perceptual one. For the individual is an infrastructural barrier to perception, so that it seems that one would be able to place their personal realm upon perceptual data and thus desynchronize its organic pattern.

It might seem the same, that of infrastructural separation to perceptual data and that of personal projection upon it, but there is one tenet that is the cause of its disruption. Because all perceptual data is based on a manifestation of the psychological state of an individual, placing the individual upon the perceptual data is, in effect, the degeneration of one's individualistic state. When infrastructure has disruptions in its synchronicity, it is because it is true that perceptual data is not applicable in a linear model, but this is not based on one's individuality. It is the case that, at a molecular level, there is synchronicity between all of nature, and disruptions are merely the exponential state of an individual in their psychological differentiation of that perceptual data.

It might seem ambiguous that one will experience a perceptual disruption based on the infrastructure, but it is the happenstance of a conceptual disparity rather than a true infrastructural dismemberment. This is why we have the case of the psychological projection upon perceptual disruption as the cause of individual degeneration because one is essentially applying their known self to the perceptual desynchronization, thus making itself aware of raw perceptual data but at the behest of the individual state. It is fundamentally self-sacrificial, and this is what we have termed in other works as domesticating consciousness.

There are many ways that one can arrive at the juncture of placing their personal realm upon the perceptual data, and one of its chief attributors is a lack of method towards general perceptual data. When we discuss the notion of having a method towards perceptual data, it is merely the gain of access to a perceptual data stream for whatever reason, to then have no level of individual apparatus that approaches the subject as though it is a subject. It is rather outside the notion of being a discipline and foremost a complete existential drowning.

Without this method or apparatus to approach the perceptual data, upon experiencing perceptual desynchronization, which is more than usual both infrastructurally and psychologically, one would naturally be disposed to the projection or input of their psychological state upon that very infrastructure. For what would halt the process of one projecting their psychological state on their perceptual data if not a mediator or an apparatus that approaches the subject from the onset?

We could ask the question of how one can approach or be exposed to the perceptual data when they have no apparatus to the subject, and this can be answered by the prevalence of data streams that have been made available for anybody who participates in its infrastructural center bases, which is unusual as a historical precedent but prevalent in the contemporary era.

Historical precedent had the encampment and engagement of the process to approach the perceptual data stream, and by this effect, it is only those who have socially proved themselves to be tenable of an apparatus who thus gained entry into the perceptual data stream of that level. However, this was a historical mistake of the psychological continuity of an individual or of the general nature of infrastructure, for in the attempt at gating the perceptual data and effect, it is that they differentiated themselves against the very access to the data stream. Thus, they have locked themselves out of that access but have promoted themselves as the entranceway into the realm by which one can gain access to the perceptual data stream, despite the fact that it is completely unavailable to that which is least accessible by nature of perceptual process. For this very reason, and this ambiguity amongst the populace or citizens, it was both a measure of control and disingenuousness, by the fact that the populace viewed the most gated, least successful arenas as the perceptual center, all the while those least accessible still remained as the high point or uppermost tier to which one would strive. In this way, one was motivated to gain access to the apparatus or modality to approach the perceptual data so as to gain the social tier that would give them access to these least accessible arenas. Therefore, it was both to the benefit of society and to its detriment, the benefit of motivating the populace towards an apparatus of perceptual data but deprived of the final access to that domain, since the uppermost tier was of least accessibility and least availability to perceptual data.

Most of civilized history can be accounted for in this format, but then there were events that differentiated from this approach and instead did not propose the least accessible arenas as the uppermost tier of perceptual data. In this way, the detriment to society was the very notion that one need not have an apparatus to approach perceptual data because of the very fact that it did not motivate the ladder of development towards modalities that would finally give them access, for the accessibility was open to all. The benefit is that one need not go far to gain its access, but as the alternative would be without an apparatus or modality towards the subject, it thereby caused the detriment that we are in discussion about.

To alleviate the detriment, one would be required to follow a system, whether individually or as a group, that orders a development of an apparatus towards the perceptual data stream despite no incentive to do so. The incentive of yesteryear in this process would have been to gain ascendancy towards the social hierarchy to finally approach the assumed center of perceptual data. There is no perceptual incentive, or social one, for that matter, in the claim for ascendancy because it is readily accessible for all, and there is no reason to develop an apparatus towards the subject other than for the appreciation of psychological and infrastructural health of development.

The social realm cannot even offer an incentive to this apparatus since it does not exemplify itself as anything more than a receptacle of the already available perceptual data. It is almost as if the social hierarchy is considered arbitrary in its proposition, since it is but a makeup of individuals that have the same level of access as anyone else, with no general or genuine nature of a social hierarchy in this realm. For what makes one individual higher than the other if perceptual data is accessible to all, and the only token that may be had is the ability of access to the apparatus, such that it would almost be the one who is most distant from perceptual data who becomes the representation of themes and the cause of hierarchical status.

A social mistake may be made to assume that there is a social hierarchy in obtaining access to the perceptual data, and this is only because all individuals have gained or have been able to gain access to it and find themselves in a state of degeneracy or detriment such that it is assumed that if it is not a process and is thus not accessible, one thereby assumes that there is a tenable social hierarchy to gain that access, despite the fact that none exists.

Chapter Three: Perception and Domesticity

Section One: Domesticated Perception: On the Illusion of Form and the Architecture of Psyche Lineage

The process of domestication can be viewed as anything that delineates perceptual form in a congruent manner. This generates a comprehensive picture of domestication, where it is not solitary in a category apart from regular psyche processes, but is the container that distracts from any perceptual form. "Distraction" might be too strong of a word, but it is the avoidance of perceptual form, the lineage towards perceptual form, and the illusion of perceptual form. The domesticated process is not constituted to avoid perceptual form as an outright entity, but because of a misunderstanding or appropriation of its process, it can be viewed as embedded into perceptual form, or worse off, as the regulator and controller of all perceptual information.

Instead of gaining a definition from domestication, where we would be adept at learning its process, we should be looking at the objective of perceptual information, which coincidentally would allow us all such psyche process that does not tie into domesticated capacity. It would seem that we are let down from doing this appropriately because, in any perceptual form, it would constitute a preliminary stage of a domesticated process. A box is a perceptual form, whereas, with the connotation of home structure, which undoubtedly was made away from perceptual information, the house does not display itself as such, but rather as a structure like any other.

Even the conceptual framework of a "box" would require a preliminary domesticated capacity, particularly to allow for that information, such as the hard-wired container in contrast to the cyclical one, being less regulative without angles. Or, in a Freudian sense, the father as the original domesticated capacity for the angles of a home and its external manifestation, and the mother as the original domesticated capacity for the rounded and internal aspects. This leads us to the conclusion of our investigation, where it seems that there is no solitary perceptual form, whether the regulating angles of the "box" or the house, without its counterpart of domesticated capacity. This allows us to end the discussion before we have even gained entrance into the particulars.

First, we must address the issue at hand: although perceptual forms are, in fact, generated by domesticated capacity, they are not mutually exclusive. After the fact, when one entertains the perceptual form of house as such, there is no need for the domesticated capacity that offered its assistance. The house is viewed in its entirety as a house, despite its lineage of information gained by the domesticated capacity. In all later events, one does not require the preliminary domesticated capacity to experience that perceptual form.

And in the Freudian example, the domesticated capacity is the father and mother, pertaining to the aspects related to and representing those of the home structure. Once this gives rise to the perceptual form of a home, that domesticated capacity is not the regulating element that offers the molded image. The image that enters the perceptual realm is a compacted version of domesticated capacity that simply pointed in the direction of the external world. But once that perceptual information is taken in, the home is constituted as a singular entity, which cannot be deconstructed back into its domesticated capacity, even though it is not exclusive of that capacity.

Freudian philosophy states that one can deconstruct a perceptual form to gain entry into the domesticated capacity that composes it, but it is an illusion to believe that this construction is the full generation of the perceptual form. It is simply one aspect of the lineage of that perceptual form. Not only are there numerous other elements, especially environmental, that contribute to it, but the final perceptual form of the house is constituted as a perceptual entity in its own right, molded in itself. And the process of deconstructing it is itself a domesticated process.

The moment we enter the psyche and attempt to understand its process, we have already lost the perceptual realm. In this sense,

Freudian philosophy first builds a domesticated structure in order to deconstruct a perceptual form, but in doing so, never actually enters the perceptual form itself. It remains a secondary process.

It may nonetheless be successful, owing to the fact that domesticated capacity has developed itself to such an extent that later perceptual forms (not those of the historical precedent of what constituted a house, but forms that arise further in time from that developed state) will then take up the new molded image based on that developed capacity. This explains why the therapeutic process is an ordeal that takes months, if not years: we are not waiting to develop the best version of capacity, but rather for that capacity to take up perceptual form.

This is precisely why one cannot remove a perceptual form once it has gained entry, despite its change in the domesticated capacity. Even if we were to entertain the framework in which boxes correlate to structures, and structures constitute a home, this will not change the already-gained perceptual form of experiencing it as a house. We may use the word "experience" in a liberal sense, when in our discussion the experience is the perceptual form, not as a housed aspect of a psyche, but rather correlating to the perceptual form itself, which has no experiencer nor can be constituted as a mobile entity of the psyche.

The only change in the domesticated capacity would be to generate a more complex perceptual form, whereas it was viewed as a home, it can now, owing to its developed domesticated capacity, be viewed as a controlled environment for the habitat of developmental growth. The perceptual form of "home" was merely the placement of a constitution, but after a domesticated capacity which enabled the success of perspectives, the home is perceived with the form of that developmental arena, which is now a more complex perceptual form.

This can occur the other way around, in which one can entertain the domesticated capacity of a box, following its geometric complexities, so that the next perceptual form of the home will be viewed as a geometric form, but importantly, less of the constitutional signature of a home. It is not that the homebody is somehow less than; rather, one of the particulars that allows for that perceptual form has been developed so that now it can take a dominant stance in the final perceptual form. The domesticated capacity is simply the generation of particulars away from perceptual process that organizes sentimentality, which will finally reach a verdict in a molded perceptual form.

A veteran architect might very often fail to envision the constitution of structures without the very domesticated capacity of architectural tradition, so that the final perceptual form is viewed in relation to that tradition. It is, of course, possible for the architect to develop the domesticated capacity of both the constitution of a homebody and structures in general, so that it will be embedded into the perceptual form to counterbalance the more sophisticated version of other elements that allow for the final form.

Again, we are only speaking from the vantage point of a domesticated process, for the entire modality of science and philosophical inquiry is based on a domesticated capacity. So that when we discuss something's embedded perceptual form, it is only based on the arena we have reconstructed, for the perceptual form itself has no embeddedness, because it is the full experience of nature as a stamp on the psyche that does not bear a lineage, for it is a creation of itself. Similar to a child, who is considered an entity of itself, despite the fact that we can attribute a certain form of lineage to their genealogy, but only in the sense of the discipline of genealogy or paternal perspectives. From the vantage of the child, lineage is not necessarily the only direction to constitute their existence, but rather they are an organic form that is processing itself. And so when we give it the offering of a lineage, it is merely a domesticated experience of such, and not the perceptual form or external form of the child, as we would never say the child is the father, but rather resembles the father. The resemblance is based on an external party taking perspective on the cause, rather than the mending of two external forms and agents.

We can then enter into a clause: if the architect does not counterbalance the other elements that give rise to the perceptual form of the structure, they will inevitably lose that capacity in all later perceptual forms. In some sense, this compels the architect into a journey through all domesticated capacities that lead up to the perceptual form of a structure, or else to lose those elements altogether.

Domesticated Capacities and the Authentic Perceptual Form

What is interesting about domesticated capacities is how they fortify themselves as a criteria of informational paddles that allow for continuous dissemination and disintegration. It disseminates its internal information to offer itself in constant motion to perceptual forms, without negating its own process as facilitating that regard. It also facilitates the fact of disintegration and sets itself as a criterion to reflect on other domesticated capacities and perceptual forms themselves.

It conflicts with other domesticated capacities to rule out a final perceptual form, which is the amelioration of the most pronounced elements of each domesticated capacity. It also disintegrates the possibility of perceptual form, for example, in the case where one is met with a high-exposure perceptual event, to which it will draw back on domesticated capacities to give and allow a sequence to interpret the data, or to mold it into a perceptual form. In that process, it will attempt to disenfranchise what would be the case of a performative perceptual form.

If one relinquishes the process of seeking out a domesticated capacity for a perceptual form, then it will take the natural course of molding the image, as it were, facilitated by a domesticated lineage but not regulated or controlled by it. The differences between the two are vast: in one, it is the domesticated capacity that is influencing and in some ways setting the criteria for the entire perceptual form; in the other, it is the perceptual form that acknowledges its entity as a separate and unique experience, drawn from a domesticated capacity without seeking out that interpretation, meaning it is the most rudimentary perceptual form.

The final product is a perceptual form that is not directed, regulated, or integrated with domesticated capacity. In the case where the perceptual form does seek out a domesticated capacity, it does so as a multi-image of itself, to which the domesticated capacity did facilitate, influence, and regulate, but all from the sidelines, so that the perceptual image, in its final case, is still its own unique form.

However, the major difference is the fact that in this case, the domesticated capacity was sought out in solitary motion in a strict direction, instead of the amelioration of all natural processes of domesticated elements that reach toward the perceptual form.

In the case of a psychopath, the domesticated forms take precedence in the perceptual forms, but uniquely so, and rather are most preliminary and rudimentary toward the perceptual form. If we were to deconstruct that perceptual form, we would still find the domesticated capacity, as in any perceptual form. In this case, it is unique in that it has not been molded by a specific direction of a domesticated capacity. More so, all the previous domesticated capacities have already been relieved of their duty in the psyche, so that it is deconstructed and defragmented to a point where very little domesticated capacity assists in continuing perceptual forms; although there are going to be domesticated capacities that will retain some semblance because of their rudimentary nature in the developmental stage of the psyche.

In the case of the highly domesticated individual, because they have and contain a vast array of domesticated capacities, or to use an example, they contain a multitude of "homes", when they reach the outside of these homebodies, they retain all of this information to direct the perceptual form in a very specific and intended manner. This is most profound, but also most untrue to the perceptual form as it is deserving without these domesticated perspectives.

The genuine perceptual form is that which is without any domestication or domesticated capacities that provide nuance and direction. But that genuine form is also unsophisticated since it does not have a direction of discourse to reach into that form. So, although it is most profound precisely because of the domestic context, or the homebound state, from which one reaches outward, it is also the case that the perceptual form is not being received according to its proper justification.

Populations view kings, leaders, and major political structures through a highly directed lens, one that can be attributed to an over-domesticated capacity. As a result, the perceptual form, comprising simple infrastructure and what the organic body perceives in relation to other organic structures is neglected in favor of reinforcing this intensified experience of domestication.

In the case of the psychopath, whatever domesticated capacity exists is continually negotiated away from its foundation; they do not draw from a domesticated reserve. Their perceptual forms are, in fact, in their most genuine state. Yet, among psychopaths who engage in antisocial behavior, there remains a minimal resemblance of domestication, which they seek to resolve by attaining the full perceptual form. They attempt this by destroying the few domesticated elements preserved in memory, in order to achieve that final form. In this way, their laughter, the cruel aftermath, signifies their joy in being able to reject and annihilate the remnants of domesticated capacity within the psyche, thereby completing the perceptual form that arises momentarily after the act of injustice.

The point of the matter is that domesticated capacities do not dissolve into the psyche out of habit and remove their influence, but rather retain their entire structure, since they are an informative reserve for perceptual form. The matter of removing the domesticated capacity is in recognizing its illegitimate stance as informative to perceptual form. It is illegitimate because never has a perceptual form been imprinted by domesticated capacity; rather, it has been influenced in a direction to give a certain form. As we have noted, it is not embedded in the form of that domesticated capacity.

The domesticated capacity only serves to give a direction to the perceptual form, which can be to the detriment of, first and foremost, other domesticated capacities (for this is one of near-infinite processes by which one can approach a perceptual form), and second, to the distraction of the perceptual form itself, which in its genuine format does not require nor need a domesticated direction.

In the most extreme case, the division between the domesticated capacity and the perceptual form is blurred—due to the fact that the individual preserves the perceptual form as if it were based on that domesticated lineage, despite the very true fact that no perceptual form can be directly connected to its domesticated capacity. Although it is true that the influence is there, it gives direction to the form rather than serving as the basis of the form itself. If we uncover the details of any perceptual form, especially in cases where there is a widely unrealistic conjecture of domesticated capacity, we can realize that the perceptual form still retains its original, genuine format. It has only been refocused and vitalized toward the specific domesticated capacity.

For example, the perceptual form of a house will always be based on its genuine nature. The constitution, which is a conceptual overlay of a house since it is simply a structure at its fundamental level, is still a conjecture of that perceptual form. And even as we assert that it is a house, there is still leeway between that and its genuine perceptual form. However, if we dig deeper, the structure is itself a domesticated capacity, and there is a more genuine form than "structure"—which is the division between geographical space. In this way, it is the truest perceptual form, because the existence of an individual is also separated from geographical space. There is no requirement of a domesticated capacity to ascertain that perceptual form, due to the happenstance of subjective experience.

However, one can lose that subjective experience, so that even the concept of structures as separated geographical space loses its animation. One begins to notice the form in openness as if it were not a structure, but rather more land that continues onward in different directions. The basis is thus constituted upon the identity of personhood, which can also be understood as a domesticated process. Yet the notion of identity asserts itself as a biological experience, wherein one perceives oneself as an individual distinct from space, as an identity of personhood, but also as an existential experience.

Thus we reach the conclusion that it is only in the manner in which one existentially attaches to anything that there is a possibility of perceptual form, all the while it is not a domesticated process to existentially attach but rather a physiological and psychological collusion. When one notices themselves as separate from the environment, and then proceeds by identifying themselves as such and thereby grounding their existence in that criterion, all else will continue in that structure, particularly amongst them is perceptual forms. That existential attachment of the idea that was first constituted is not in itself a domesticated process, but more so a biological experience, albeit based on psychological development.

Domesticated capacity retains its concealed nature unless drawn upon by the perceptual form. The associations of that form, based on its prior process of generation, has one meet that domesticated capacity. The house, when engaged in perceptual form, will entice all the domicile states in relation to that, whether dormant, underdeveloped, or repressed. The level of profundity toward that perceptual form will be in accordance with those associated capacities which give it that language. If one actualizes that house or that moment in perception of the house, those domicile capacities will be extracted to give detail to that form.

In the regular case, the house would be simple enough of a form, to which only those capacities that are more general will suffice as an association. For instance, the father might be the preliminary capacity to the house structure, but will not be brought to bear in every case of that perceptual form, although when it is perceived with added vitality, it would exact that capacity amongst others.

However, when there is a development at stake, where those capacities are not in their original state, such that one develops the notion in relation to the "father," then when that profound perceptual form of the house takes effect, that new form of domesticated capacity will be received as part of that process. As of that moment, the perceptual form known as the house will now be associated with that new capacity, and the antiquated version will have little to no effect upon that form. It still remains a domesticated capacity that participated in the innovative development, but as the development goes along, those will be replaced. This is the primary intention of psychoanalytical theorists, in which that domicile development will overtake its earlier forms by the new form of the perceptual information. However, another perceptual form can retract such and reach into the olden capacity since the integration was not thorough.

Change in its entirety only occurs when that capacity is disintegrated as a modality of perspective, in which it is found in its illegitimacy as a participant of the perceptual form. One may view the house without the connotation of the "father," since that capacity is disenfranchised owing to its domesticated process, which, in the case of this example, is difficult because of the network that such an endeavor must embark upon to perform such a deed.

In seeing how the mind's own beliefs harden into subjective laws of cause and effect, we must now examine how those beliefs likewise shape the very raw data of perception.

A perceptual form has difficult access from a domesticated base because domesticity takes over the apparatus of personhood, and especially emotional ascendancy. This perceptual form is congruent with every domesticated process. Despite our recognition of where it refers back upon, it can be assured that there is a perceptual form that generates and finalizes domesticated constructs. When one is in incongruence with a perceptual form, there is no recognition other than its most subjective possible experience, and the only manner in which it is regulated is through a domesticated foreground. The form of perception is objective, that is, the socially agreed recognition of what it constitutes, but still is possible to gain access to its substructure through an awareness of what to be on the lookout for, and any capacity by which to receive that perceptual information.

These two elements are the only regulations of a perceptual form: first, an awareness of the depth of that objective perceptual form; and second, the capacity to receive a more coherent version of the perceptual form based on a domesticated foreground. This capacity is simply the lineage of domesticity that has surrounded similar and corresponding perceptual forms, so that now, in some sense, more information can be received because of a backlog of already received information. Since the psyche retains so many data points in regard to the perceptual form based on its preliminary domesticated process, it is now in a position to take heed of the form for greater comprehension and comprehensiveness.

Take the child, for example. Because their domesticated process has only begun its initiation, when they gain access to a perceptual form, it does not have preliminary data to correlate and therefore will be perceived at the most simplistic version that parallels the state of the psyche at that moment.

We could then perceive the fashion designer, who makes it their work to refine perception toward color. Because of their constant and developing domesticated process derived from earlier perceptual forms and education, their basis of color perception is far more complex due to the background that grants the capacity to see further forward.

The first point, in which perceptual data is able to be comprehended based on a domesticated process, is not merely about the background data that has been integrated into the system through domestication, but more so because one has the knowledge of what area should be the focus of perception. Until the moment of perception occurs, it is still a domesticated system, so that when that perceptual form takes credence, it does so based on the direction that the domesticated system points toward. Once the perceptual form has already been perceived, it is too late to direct the domesticated system, because it is no longer domesticated but rather a perceptual form that must follow its own credence based on what was already developed, it is now an independent process.

This independence of the perceptual form is worthy of inquiry. Although, as noted, it is based on and influenced by the preliminary state of domesticity, its form follows a different path. This would not be engineered by the individual but by sociality, consciousness, and infrastructure, which lead toward its objective direction despite individuality. The objection of an individual can only occur after the perceptual form has been activated; in the interim, it is placed upon the psyche without alteration. If one receives a perceptual form from a certain sociality, it will, in kind, be embedded upon their psyche, and protest will not succeed in alleviating that imprint. Many times, one will conjure the opposing domestication in an attempt to undermine the perceptual form by agreeing to its opposite, but that is only a sleight of hand.

Chapter Four: Laws on Mind's Self-Reference

Causation is a perplexing phenomenon, and one often misconstrued to the point where it remains in obscurity, buried under philosophical debates and complications; so much so that the onlooker is replaced by the paradox of the universe. Although paradoxes do exist, such as the individual being both themselves and part of a broader universe, causation is not one of those paradoxes. We will now approach the subject to inquire its details.

Causality is the determinate stature of the subjective state of a single point, which is proclaimed to entertain the next point. First and foremost, whenever we proclaim causality as if it were an objective state, it is a misuse of words, for there is no such concept as causality unless we have a perpetuator of causation. Systems or broader spectrums are not embedded with causality, but rather with dynamical forces, within which any attributes could be fitted to the succeeding attributes.

If we speak of, for instance, causality of dust appearing on a windowsill, we must inquire as to the perpetuator of that causation. If we assume, implicitly, that there is an inertia preventing the appearance of dust from the very beginning of existence, then we are conflating the concept of 'causality' with the more fundamental question of existence itself. We can ascertain a near-infinite set of dynamical forces that allowed for the dust to appear on the windowsill, none more consequential than our noting the dust itself, to which our attention is part and parcel of the entire enterprise of inquiring into how the dust appears. If we do not have specific attention toward that aspect of inquiry, then we cannot inquire; for that reason, preceding the entire inquiry is the inquiry into how we have made the inquiry, into what mechanisms have been applied, by which we then recede into the mechanisms which have been applied in a near-infinite backlog.

The general causality of dust appearing on a windowsill would be attributed to a perpetuator of causality, thereby ensuring that there is a container of causation toward that causality. This container is required by two bylaws: one, that it must be subjective; and two, that it must be a container. Already we have asserted the first law: that there is no such thing as objective causality, but rather that all causality has an implicit marker of a perpetuator of causation.

These two bylaws are required because, if we do not have a subjective criterion, then it leads to a lack of complicity with a perpetuator, whereby causality remains as such and not in proportion to a perpetuator. The second law is that it must be a container, not only subjective in nature but also one that holds the material necessary for causation. It cannot be merely a medium of causality that lacks any innate or intrinsic material, even if that material is arbitrary.

Thus, we can never say that dust appearing on a windowsill belongs to the realm of causality, but rather existing alongside a perpetuator which has caused the dust to be on the windowsill. Beyond identifying this perpetuator, we must recognize that it is not a solitary agent, but rather the subjective state of the perpetuator. We could dictate that the wind caused the dust to appear on the windowsill, but still, we require the subjective modality of the wind to enable that sequence. For if we look at the wind as an objective form, not implicit with any particular material of possibility toward causation, we never arrive at the proclamation of it causing something. In other terms, it must be personalized as a subjective force, as if the wind has a modality of causation by which it caused the dust to appear on the windowsill.

Besides this, we must also assume that wind has elements within it that differ from what precedes it. What is the causation that allows wind to exist, as well as what proceeds from it; its activity in relation to the dynamical force causing the dust to settle? There must be material specific and innate to wind, contained within it, that can have the effect of causation.

We can follow this sequence to understand how these laws come into effect by approaching the subject from another angle. We could just as well say that the windowsill is the cause of the dust upon it, and we rely on it to be the perpetuator of this causation. But it is accompanied as a perpetuator, it is also subjective to our inquiry, meaning that we are asking what it would be like to be a windowsill; a constructed structure capable of being a causative factor for dust settling upon it.

More than that, it must have materiality within its construction that contains the elements specific to this causation, such that no other form has the same ability, and therefore proceeds on to a final causality. The reason we are more inclined to say that the wind caused the dust, rather than the windowsill itself, is because we apply the subjective modality of the wind in a more personalized manner than we do for a windowsill. The wind has a higher symbolic nature than the inert collection of atoms that comprise a windowsill, as well as greater mobility, whereas the windowsill is stagnant. It is simply that one seems more personable as a subjective modality for contemplation than the other, but this does not make either more or less valid in terms of causality.

To follow the point further, we will entertain more junctures of inquiry. Even the dust itself could be the cause of its own appearance on the windowsill. The perpetrator of the dust is its own nature, to which it has material contained within it to allow for its appearance. We see that it is not limited to the mere differentiation between objects (e.g., that the wind is different than the dust and thus can be the cause), but rather that even dust itself can be the cause of dust appearing, by the fact that it is both the perpetuator of its own existence and substantial material that permits a direction of causality.

Thus, we do not have any liminal data by which one form is more causative than another; wind, construction, or dust itself. If we follow disjointed logic of negation, we could say that without the wind, the dust would not appear; without the construction, the dust would not appear, and without dust, dust would not appear.

One more stretch, although this can go on this route to near-infinite proportions, we could also say that the appearance of the dust on the windowsill is the perpetuator of that causation. For the appearance contains the material that allows for the dust to appear, thereby allowing even the verb of 'the dust appearing' to be a possible cause. By the same negating logic, without the possibility of appearance, there would be no dust appearing on the windowsill.

Therefore, we conclude that causality is never an objective form, but rather the subjective experience of causation, or of the perpetuator of causality and its contained material. Besides these three elements, there is a fourth: the final causation. In our case, the final causation is the dust appearing on the windowsill, but more than that, it is the application of the dust appearing on the windowsill. For there is no inquiry into x upon y unless we care about its applicable form. Even as an example, the dust appearing on the windowsill is the applicable form by which we conceptualize dust, windowsill, and their interaction.

Meaning to say, there is no study of causality unless there is an objective for the causation to be implied upon. We have not offered the implication of the dust appearing on the windowsill explicitly, but we have done so subliminally. When we use this as an example, the implication is its modality as a use case for performance. Therefore, the direction of causation toward its implication is meant to serve as the exemplified form that renders our inquiry coherent.

We are only concerned with wind or construction as perpetrators of causality because we want to assist in the exemplification of the example. But in the implicated form of one who is genuinely inquiring into the presence of dust on a windowsill, it must be implicated in some form. It could be that the dust must be cleaned, or that its cause must be understood because it creates a disturbance. We cannot inquire into causality unless we care about the value of that causation, and that value is where we inhabit the subjective state of causation.

Notice that the first perpetrator we used was wind. Implicit in our choosing that subjective modality is our value-implication: we want to ascertain the source in order to stop its disturbance. Once we understand that it is the wind, we can approach the subject more easily. There would be little purpose in understanding the subjective modality of the windowsill's construction in relation to that causation because it would not significantly aid us in setting aside the disturbance caused by the dust.

Meaning to say, if our implication were understanding of building materials and how they cohabit with dust, we would not approach the subjective mode of wind, but immediately that of building materials because that is the final implication. Therein lies the subjective modality we wish to inhabit for that implication. It is the motivation and intention of the entire subject. Therefore, any inquiry into causation must have a fourth bylaw: the implicated factor will determine the specific subjectification of the perpetuator of causality.

Reception of a form of potential or substantiation is only due through a strategic process, which, if any of the steps are divergent, the end result would be a misguided apprehension of that substantiation. The first of its processes is mirroring or embodying the state without any requisite material between the entity and the element of substantiation, in which it is of the degenerate form that copycats and mirrors the process without any deviation other than calibrating the neurological sequences in spite of any conceptual database. The only conceptual aspect of that stage is the initial decision of the specific entity to mirror. Thus, it is the case that it is usually the general citizen who will attempt to mirror the upper strata because they are deemed such by the general public without much conceptual analysis.

Because the conceptual analysis is lacking based on the entire sequence of the process, is almost arbitrarily decided as to what will be constituted as an entity of substantiation for the stage to begin its procedure. There are going to be general entities that will be foremost on the list of a socially developed being, such as parental figures and societal figures, because these are the most pressing dramatic imprints of potential, one by the personalized aspect and the other by recognition of the public sphere. After that initial period of mirroring the procedural process of the entity of substantiation, there is then the separation between the two parties. For if there is a continuing basis of embodiment in such mirroring, there is no element of individuation that will succeed in the conceptual information that underlies the entire form of potential.

It is after the fact a conceptual endeavor despite the mirroring being mostly a process of sensations and neurological computation, it is based on an initial appreciation of a conceptual objective. Even in the chimp's accession to the dominant chimp, it will be in accordance with an initial agreement of a conceptual objective that is tied with hierarchy and domination. After the circumstance, it proceeds to the highest intelligent mammal, as it is the one most imprinted with this process, due to its beginning stages of seeking conceptual understanding, which makes the process of higher life forms possible.

Therefore, we have the important step in the process of separation between the mirroring stage and the accession to the conceptually formed underpinning that lays dormant in the substantiation. We can access, at the point of separation, which is attached to that form of embodiment and the substantiation that goes along with it, and in doing so, will find correlation to the embodied apparatus of that substantiation. This is made possible through the very notion that reserves descending into the individual apparatus to contrast with data points. If the separation is not coordinated between the individual and the substantiation, it will not succeed in descending into the personal realm and consequently available to contrast itself with the internal apparatus that approached the embodied interactivity.

This is the most pressing stage in its fully required stature because it is after the idolization of the initial entity, being against one's nature to existentially separate from that endeavor. For one must find in themselves the mode of individual commitment that does not ideate the prior state; thus a required accessibility towards the arbitrariness of the very thing they have sought to recreate for themselves. Moreover, if they do so with an existential separation, there will be little motivation for the third stage of coordination. Despite the fact that the internal apparatus of mirroring was completed, the contrast between the personal self and that internal apparatus is distinctly separated, and there is little correlation or coordination, despite it being a true part of selfhood.

We constantly forget that subjectification is not a mechanism in itself but rather as part of the implicating factor. It is the value judgment after the fact that creates the initial subjectification in the first place. Irwin D. J. Brass, in Design for a Decision, notes: "The difficulty arises when the purpose of the decision is stated broadly. The problem of measuring desirability has been sadly neglected by science. It is admittedly an [arduous] topic to tackle, but it is a job that will have to be done." Later on, he says: "When action has only a single outcome, the desirability of the outcome may also be regarded as the desirability of action, and causes the value system."xx

The implication of causality must be embedded in the subjectification of the perpetrator because we are searching; much like a justice system investigating a criminal, for the already implicated measure that now requires a lineage of responsibility. We are beginning from the implicated stature. We do not start from the subjectification of wind, but rather from the implicating measure of having dust appear on a windowsill, to which we then trace back through a lineage of responsibility otherwise termed 'the perpetrating causation', based on the already existing value system of what we intend to implicate and what we desire.

If we desire to reduce the amount of dust on window sills, then the subjectification of the perpetrator, known as the wind, would be a shorthand for that process. Therefore, we need to "blame" the wind so that we can function within its modality, understand its material, and utilize that information to obtain a better outcome.

Generally, all notions of causation lead back to justice systems, for they rely heavily on the subjectification of causation in their need to trace the implication of a crime back to a perpetrator; in order to make its lineage known. If we study justice thoroughly, we understand that it is, in many ways, arbitrary. There is the subjectification of the criminal as the causative agent, when in fact the justice department attributes that causality to the perpetrator. This attribution removes ambiguity from the implication of criminality.

This is highlighted dramatically in the case of vehicle manslaughter, and especially in the case of inebriation, to which, within a system of causality, we would not necessarily attribute the modality of recklessness or inebriation as the perpetrator of the final outcome. But in the justice case, it is such a perspective. For already, the implication of the justice system in the case of vehicle dilemmas is to recognize the lineage of authority to a complex force of mechanisms, so as to alert a responsibility token that does not necessarily align with the direct implication of the final outcome. This differs, for example, from homicide, where the implicating factor is the recognition of the personal aspect and the causation of homicidal acts.

This is not the case for vehicle manslaughter, because we are not studying or reflecting upon human or social modality, but rather on the necessary recognition of a role that a person would take, despite the lineage being ambiguous since many dynamic forces are at play, such as the entire construction of having set up a vehicle within infrastructure bound to inevitable failures. That would be the perpetrator of causation, if we were to view it as we would a homicidal act. In such a view, we would remove the case scenarios of causations that lead to vehicle manslaughter, to which the entire enterprise of vehicles is the path of least resistance. It is only the case that the justice system, in its values and implications of such an outcome, would rather behold a personal addendum, for it is regularly processing this matter in other areas of the court. Consequently, it is no stretch to continue such intention in that direction, despite the lineage being arbitrary.

Because the justice system is most adapted to human or social responsibility, the natural perpetrator will always lead back to the human mechanism, despite the purpose of the implication being to proceed with social order in a better fashion based on current outcomes. The final implication is that of making sense of, and assigning personal obligation to, criminality. Although this may deviate from one justice system to another, it remains sufficiently consistent that the subjectification of the criminal fits the necessary mold. We want to inhabit the criminal because we seek to engineer a form of reconciliation, a personal recognition of selfhood, of which the subjectification of a human being is the first step.

We would not want to re-objectify weather patterns on the day of the criminal act, because we do not wish to develop a deeper understanding of meteorology, but rather of personal development in relation to causation and criminality. It is with this assistance that we come to understand the lineage of criminality in a way that can have a recognizable effect on oneself. For one is much like another, and therefore can fit the reflection that may deviate from further acts of criminality, if reflected upon accordingly.

It is arbitrary that the criminal was the perpetrator of causation, if not for this implicated value. When that implicated value changes, for example, when a non-citizen is the perpetrator, we notice a different approach to the lineage of that criminality. In such a case, the focus shifts to the broader subject of a "foreigner" rather than to social reflection. Since non-citizens are not part of the class system, they do not carry the same implication of reflection upon the regular citizen, and thus would not produce that same undue effect.

A crucial philosophical debate of the last millennium is very much tied up with causation, and reflects not so much upon philosophical discourse, but rather a disheartening misunderstanding of causation. Freedom only becomes a questionable item when it encroaches upon causation, which we have already established relies on an implication value rather than a metaphysical system. It is not so much a question of free-will as it is of value associations and the subjectification of the perpetrator of causality that sums up the affair.

The decision is based on the recognition of subjectification in accordance with its causal chain. The general question would be: does one have free-will to do good or evil? But it is the very question that notates the implicated value, that of attempting good and avoiding evil, to which there is a causal linkage back to the perpetrator that does evil or subsequent good.

The question then becomes: is the subjectification of oneself as the perpetrator of good or evil enough of a mentality to control the outcome? The answer is based on the broader environment, to which that subjectification is mostly arbitrary. For if one does not understand good or evil, then being a perpetrator of any form of activity would cause a lineage of causation that is arbitrary. Meaning to say: understanding itself is another perpetrator of that causal link, as well as the environment to which good and evil are placed, and so on and so forth, among the near-infinite perpetrators of causality.

The very notion of free-will is to place the subjectification of the perpetrator onto oneself, as if they are the seed of their activity, to which the value contract of good and evil is then processed. It is more substantial as a form of self-accounting than anything else, as it has a judicial implication, for it is the subjectification of the person as the causal link only to accounting, and thus to endow a self-recognition process through which begins a development of sequences for the psyche, all based on that guilt-ridden modality that eventually leads them away from the path of activity.

Philosophical notation of whether man has free will is merely the self-accounting of placing one at the responsible helm toward the causal link in the implication of morality. It is not a philosophical question, but rather a process of accounting with arbitrary guilt, upon which one hopes to build themselves from such a predicament. It is fundamentally Christian, in that guilt is first embedded into the system despite any development or procedure, so as to then deal with that disproportionate experience of disruption. This, in turn, provides the vitality to rebuild, or in this case, to first build a structure and sequence that formats that guilt in a manner that would avoid an eventual outcome at a later stage.

It is taking upon oneself the indebtedness, almost like borrowing before building, onto which the entire debt already creates the sequence and motivation to perform the deed of building. It is arbitrary in a sense, just like one who takes a loan for a project: the loan is arbitrary in the nature of money or currency and does not connect to the project. But the inevitable subjective experience of that indebtedness to the bank has one motivated toward the construction of the project to its finality— more so than ever having begun the process in the first place. This is not fundamentally philosophical, for causality or causation is arbitrary. But it is a process of development, and in its origin, probably a Christian process of development, with its benefits and disadvantages accordingly.

Mind and Itself

process of development, with its benefits and disadvantages accordingly.

Chapter Five: Psychology of Mind's Self Reference.

Section One: Acceptance, Enclosure, and the Vulnerable Comprehensiveness of the Psyche

Acceptance is the key concept in differentiating between interactive specificity and comprehensive sociality of the psyche. In the case of the ladder, where one faces inaccessibility to the infusion of the circuit without an irregular inhibition, would be the case that there is no need for acceptance; for that is the ultimate comprehensiveness and therefore is not a limiting factor of the psyche or its parallel environment. Acceptance then becomes a factor when one is not in excess ability to pervade the psyche, but rather such that whatever the interaction, it would be noticed as disruptive to the regular state of affairs, and therefore would beckon acceptance parameters so as not to find oneself at the border between that interactive state of affairs and regular permeability.

According to the interactive encapsulation, it is a pronounced reality with the rest of the psyche as merely its backdrop which has no effect or direction to its happenstance. We can already perceive the difficulty when there is an absence of acceptance to its domain, whereby it does not correlate to permeability, nor so to the interactive specificity, and in this vacuity one enables the experience of the comprehensive psyche but still more so without direct access, in addition to the fact that the availability of residing in the interactive pocket is diminished by its lack of adherence.

With this disparity in place, one has the vitality of the comprehensive psyche without its intricate material. Instead, there is an interaction from the vantage of the interactive stance towards that comprehensiveness, which has one reflect the entirety of the psyche in its vulnerability. The reflection occurs because one is at the seat of perspective that can look down upon the psyche, but does so in a manner of its vulnerability. Although we would like to have the reflection take a neutral tone upon the psyche, due to the interactive enclosure, it compels the reflection to be in what way comprehensiveness does not permeate that very enclosure.

By being in the enclosure, which is part and parcel of the psyche, it exemplifies itself as without merit of the comprehensiveness of the psyche, for why would it enable the ability of enclosure if not for the fact that the comprehensiveness is not as comprehensiveness as thought to be? Almost like a child, to which without a notion of love from their parents, takes the perspective that they are flawed to some degree, for if love was true and sophisticated, it would reach their state of experience, and when it does not, it is either the case of self-degeneration or parental misgivings.

From this example we might infer that the interactive pocket can reflect not necessarily on the misgiving of that comprehensiveness but that somehow the interactive stance is fundamentally broken, for if not, it would be receptive to that comprehensiveness. While this can also be the circumstantial reflection, it still would have one reflect the comprehensiveness of the psyche, or in the case of the child, the comprehensiveness of the parental figure, all from a vantage point that is above the internal experience, but views in a manner of their stance within the system. By being within the system, in the case of the child, for being part of the family body, it behests the reflection to be in how this interactive stance, or role in the family body, is detracted from the comprehensiveness.

This would automatically take the perspective in how that detraction took place, for that is the predicament that had allowed this possibility of reflection from being an ability despite the prevalence of being within the system. Subsequently, the child then reflects the parents in their vulnerability, for the credence to have them reflect in any manner with the parents is their seclusion from them, and in this way they are seen in how very much they are flawed as a comprehensive system. Although that reflection could take on a detailed analysis based on the sophistication of the reflection, it will fundamentally be based on the inquiry of its vulnerability. The same is found in the interactive pocket, where the reflection on the rest of the psyche will be bound to the fact of its vulnerability as a comprehensive system.

There is an external superego and an internal one, and an understanding of how they operate within their respective modalities would offer clarity to their utility and procedure in regulating the regular will of the psyche and general sociality. General sociality would be defined by the normal experience of the psyche, were it not for a superego impediment. In the case of structuralism, it would be the separation of space to a point where conceptual connections do not serve a translucent continuum, so that one side would be general sociality and the other a formalization of a superego.

All internal superegos have found their lineage in an external source, and it is this recreation that formalizes it as an internal superego. The reason for this recreation are as follows: so long as the superego remains external, it will sit above the psyche like an overlord, to which there is no interaction with the superego, nor is there an ability to formalize something unique for the psyche that is not in approximation of that superego. It is, in some sense, a full subordination, and there is no individualization beyond the details of that superego.

There is, however, an interaction with the superego itself, not as an individualized perspective of the happenstance, but more so the embodiment and objective realization of that figure. We can understand this in the case of something political, to which it is fairly objective as to what is considered such, and it is not upon individuals to differentiate that. This objective realization is the imbued sentimentality of the superego as experienced by general sociality, and importantly not by an individual process. This is why the individual does not really have a considerable interaction with the external superego, as it is only the represented political experience of its figuration, with which they do not interact but rather embody.

Could one distinguish a dimension of the superego that depends on general sociality for the very formation of the traits we recognize as constituting it? If it is, in fact, a political experience or something imbued by a general consensus, it will be reliant and dependent upon sociality for its definition. For example, in some societies the dominating figure is one with access to wealth; in other societies, it is the one who has access to courage, so that if there is an attempt at a superego in a society based on courage but embodies a sense of wealth, it will not be organized as a dominion to general sociality because it is not constituted as a controlling factor.

Despite the fact that we can find that there is a lineage between wealth and control of personage because it is not realized in general society it will not constitute as a formalized superego. There are a thousand and one ways by which one single character can control or regulate the formalization of all personage, but it is only that which general sociality has constituted as the superego.

This very fact gives us a realization of how the superego, as an external mechanism, is vulnerable to general sociality, to which it will only follow based on the parameters that are given to it by its objective realization. We can follow this logic into more extreme realms, in which a person controls the domicile state of another. Even in that case, it is merely based on the general realization that controlling one's domicile state is a realized superego.

Throughout history we could find societies in which it was merely an accepted norm to have one control another's domicile state, and there was no protestation, not because it was the feebleness of the subordinates, but more so because controlling another's domicile state was not viewed as a constituent superego. Other formalizations of dependency were more dominant in such societies: the one with courage, or the one with wealth, or the one with access to resources, or the one with access to power, or the one who knew how to deal with the domicile state that was being controlled by another, or the one with intelligence, and so on, so that it is the sociality that decides the constitution of a superego, to which even controlling of one's domicile state would not necessarily constitute a superego position.

We would not say that a government is a superego over individuals just because they control the exit and entering into their state, even though this would still constitute a control of movements in the domicile state, because that is not a recognized superego. It does not constitute a formal superego, but rather an experience of life that does not disrupt internal sociality or societal sociality.

This is why it is sort of ambiguity to discuss a direct formalization of a superego. For even in the case of a father, it is not merely the father's control of the child but rather in what way the superego is politicized and thus found within the father as a character upon the child. For example, in societies where controlling or regulating one's domicile state does not constitute a formal superego, if the father conducts himself as such, there would be no difference in the experience of the child's psyche. However, in a society where wealth is constituted as a formal superego, the wealthy father is automatically entered into the arena of a formal superego because that is the general consensus of society.

Thus, in contemporary times in which the wealthy individual is a formal superego, all children of wealthy parents will automatically enter into a state of realization toward their father as a superego despite whatever procedure of childhood rearing occurs. Although in the case of the father who is domineering of the domicile state of the child, it is an active participation in the creation of a superego upon the child, and in the case of the wealthy father it is merely a matter of fact, so that there is no need for activity between father and child for the creation of the superego, it is one in the same in the experience of the child's psyche.

Both cases have the experience of the superego because the constitution of the superego is based on how society represents the superego, to which it is fulfilled in both cases: one with the active creation through the father's participation, and the other as the byproduct of that creation. If society moves in a way that wealth is no longer constituted as a formal superego, then the wealthy father requires active participation in order to create the semblance of a superego for the child.

This is the answer to the general consensus that children of wealthy parents follow a procedure toward an experience of the superego despite the prevailing process of their childhood rearing. The same applies for the renowned father or the renowned family to which the father belongs: the child will follow based on the fact that society has constituted them as formal superegos based on whatever attribute they contain or represent. The child is born into the experience of that parental figure as the superego.

We are only attempting to explain how the superego itself, as a constituent figure, is not considerable as an entity of its own, but rather in how the personage embodies the general consensus of sociality. This very understanding is part of the process in which there is an internalization of the superego, through which we notice the arbitrariness of the entity known as the superego; and the external experience to which it is merely a participant of what is politically considered such.

After this knowledge, one has a less easy time being dependent on the external figure known as the superego because of its arbitrariness. One has a choice to make: either to continue communion with the external superego; allowing it to be considered a form in itself despite the realizations mentioned above, or to accept that it is a process of the psyche more than an external form, and to take the system of the superego rather than the external form and apply it to the internal psyche.

This is the advent of the child gaining maturity: instead of allowing the embodiment of the father figure to control and regulate the entire process of their general will, they decide to become the internalization of the father, not in that the father is formalized as a process upon the psyche, but rather that the awareness of how a superego operates is internalized, so that it follows a similar mechanism without the namesake of the father or whatever superego was gained from the external experience.

Think about the rift between an adolescent child and their father, where the father is exerting his superego upon the child, and the child is applying that mechanism from their internal state against that external form, so that the rift is between an external form of the superego as opposed to the newly formed internal mechanism, whose first order of business is to disrupt the external form from regulating the psyche, because they have implemented their own form of regulation based on the newly formed superego. However, it is fragile, so there is a vulnerability in recognizing that the external superego is a more competent process than whatever they have constituted at the moment.

The father is not willing to let go of the superego dominance either, for the case of his belief toward the accession of power, or for the general case, which is the realization that whatever is being internalized in the adolescent mind does not constitute a performative review that regulates or controls its internal mechanisms in a detailed and coherent manner, so that the external form is still required.

The fragile superego, whether external or internal, is one that does not encompass all of the sociality upon which it is meant to be domineering. In the case of an external superego, it does not retain domination upon all that is under it. Take the case of the wealthy individual, who will find themselves lacking superego formalization when either the wealth dissipates, loses its influential power, or if they find themselves in a case where wealth does not constitute a direct accession of social hierarchy.

We notice this readily in one who is new to the experience of wealth: immediately they use such access to pursue all of their social systems to gain accession as the formal superego; only to realize that not all cases is such the domineering state. Or in the case of a society where courage is a trait for the formalization of a superego, the accession of courage in certain experiences finds itself at a loss, such as when intellectual mediums are required.

This is a case where the socialization under the domination of the superego does not constitute a lineage back to that superego, not because the superego is fragile in its internal state, but rather because it does not meet the criteria of general sociality. Another case in which the superego itself is vulnerable is when, in the case of courage, courage is lacking; or in the case of wealth, when wealth is lacking.

A third option comes to mind, where the fragile superego is found when one does not know how to make use of the superego's formalization. For example, in an organization with its mechanisms, if one does not embody the power to control that environment, although the superego is experienced based on the objective view of that power, because they do not utilize or retrieve that superego form, it becomes fragile in its state.

This is the constant trope of rulers, who must formalize their superego upon their constituents so that it continues to disseminate amongst that sociality. Objectively, there is no change to the power of a ruler; they are not fragile in the state of their formalization, just as the wealthy individual is not fragile in the weakness of their affluence, but it is rather in how it is formalized as an experience to the subordinates of that sociality.

When the change occurs for the internalization of the superego, it would retain these very parameters. There can be a fragile internal superego, either due to that lack of subordinate regulation because there is no demarcation of that imprinting of the superego fissure. When the imprinting of the superego is felt to be lacking in psychological pain to the rest of the system, then it would be taken as less than a dominant system of affairs.

The superego fissure is necessary in order to offer formalization to the psyche's happenstance so that it is treated with reverence, and in the case of the psyche treating reverence to a specific aspect, it is only through disruption. Differing from the case of the external superego, which is treated as a formalization based on its domineering stature upon regular sociality; for the internalization of a superego, in order to gain prominence amongst the regular sociality of the psyche, it not necessarily requires domination but rather the experiential state of domination.

Because the entire experience of the psyche is a unit unto itself and therefore should not have principal separations between its parts, in order to perform the feat of separation it requires a disruption. Although there is a concept of the creation of a superego in the external form based on disruption; for example, between one city and another, still it is the case that disruption alone will not be the entire bearing for a superego, but rather domination itself.

In the case of the psyche, it cannot dominate itself unless there is already a disruption where there is differentiation between its parts. That way, it can even have the accession of domination because there is one part that is separate from another. This is the case for the external form, although it is fairly unrecognized because it is a matter of fact that one individual is separate from another individual. Therefore, their differentiation is already there, and thus the disruption coexists with such domination.

Once there is a disruption within the internalization of the psyche, such that now there are two constituent parts that are separate, a single part will automatically take upon itself the superego structure and the other to be general sociality. As in the case for all disruptions, one side will be the non-disruptive perpetuation of material, and the other will be the disruptive, innovative sequence that does not correlate with general information.

Therefore, a disruption itself is the creation of the superego, because one constituent will apply itself as the domination over the other, not because of anything other than it being the part that is disruptive to general sociality. We can apply this to the external form of the superego, in which the disruption between two socialities, meaning two individuals that are naturally disruptive to each other as a unit of coherency, will not constitute such a dynamic with one being the superego and other in service to it.

Yet, it is not because there is not an existent superego embedded in the dynamic, for every dynamic would constitute one being the superego and the other being general sociality, but because there is no process of convergence between the two. Therefore, it is disruption without general sociality. Just like two strangers in the street do not contain any sequence between each other, although there is differentiation, it is a mechanism of disruption. Thus, we call it the stranger with no sense of domicile state, meaning the non-stranger.

It is only because of a dynamic between stranger and non-stranger, or the one containing the domicile state and the other in performance to the domicile state, that we enter a union in which one is the disruptor, and one is general sociality. Therefore, every dynamic which attempts to converge will correlate with one being the superego and the other being general sociality. Parental figures are the superego; the children are general sociality. Teachers are the superego and students are general sociality, and so on. Even within friendships, it is one who performs as the superego or the disruptor upon general sociality, and the other who is general sociality.

Of course, it is possible to perform a friendship in which each is simply the similarity of the other in validation of its sequence, but it is still the case that one is the disruptor, or the embodiment of the role of differentiation between the two, and therefore does not become general sociality.

For example, in a group of four friends, there will be one who embodies the disruption or the recognized separation between each friend. Therefore, let us call such the fourth side, and thus the majority superego. Yet, it is still the case that the coinciding threesome are not in full convergence, and between them there is a disrupting force; thus, it will be called the minority superego holding. Still, we have two constitutes which are the lowest form of the superego in the coherency of the group, and one of them will be the superego of the other.

We will find this out most readily when we separate the group formation. If we take away the fourth, and thus the majority superego, what is left is the position of the minority superego amongst the three. However, it will be felt that it is less of a disrupting force and loses certain coherency of the group and will feel weakened in its formalization.

Once we remove the minority superego, we are left with the two; both are in opposition and are then compelled in having one take the role of superego for the other. This is not the usual case, because in the coherence of the group, the three friends will attempt to correlate toward the fourth superego as a subordinate clause.

Meaning to say, in the case where the majority superego is present, the minority superego already loses its attenuation because of their acceptance toward the experience of the formalization of the superego system. There is still a dissemination from the majority superego to the minority superego, where they both hold the ability to follow the majority superego, yet still a system of dissemination of the details to which they present themselves in some capacity as a superego to the other two. It is less pronounced because of their accession to the majority superego.

In the case of the remaining two, there is still a slight superego of one to the other and the assistance of dissemination. But in the coherency of the group, the minority superego, and the domination of one over the other are diminished in order to accept the coherency of the group. The group will degenerate as a unit if there is no acceptance of a majority superego, for it must be singular so that there are subordinates to a superego clause. If the minority superego takes position as the majority superego, the group separates either way.

In fact, the entire definition of a group is in the case that there is a clear demarcation of a majority superego. When such is questionable as a position, the group, as it is formerly known, will lose its unity. The prevalent bond of the unit is based on a clear disrupting force, despite the illogicality of that. What creates convergence is when there is a disrupting force that bonds whatever is subordinate to it, because if not, the subordinates themselves will differentiate and thus not be a group. They might create their own group, but still requires a disrupting force.

This is protection offered to rulers, not alone due to the representational effect of their demise being considered the cause for protection, but rather that they are the formalization of the superego which allows unity amongst the populace. In the removal of the ruler or ruling class, the rest of the constituents are at odds with each other in the interim for a new formalization of a superego. Each constituent will proceed in deference to the other until there is an agreement, to which, in the meanwhile, all members are in the hollow realm of fulfilling that superego gap. They are all in the realm of becoming or being the superego, with which we do not bear a general sociality beyond that, as all are part of a superego. The unity is found in the agreement of a superego, and differentiation occurs in the contentious realm of that vacuum.

The internalization of that process is required to be of similar measure, in that the disruption is truly disruptive and thus creates unity in the regular state of the psyche. In a certain perspective, without an internal superego or a corresponding external form, the psyche's happenstance is in a state of transcendence from itself. Although, as we mentioned, there is unity until a disruption occurs, as is the case of a co-opt, the state of transcendence disallows organization by its failure to dismember its parts.

We will notice in a co-opt that a utopian ideal usually takes precedence, or some imaginary framework, because it cannot visualize itself, being that it is unavailable for differentiation. Instead, it must conjure a fetched idea of its process, which eventually has no semblance to the true nature of its members. In the case of the psyche, a co-opt occurs in a similar manner, wherein the data of the psyche becomes unavailable to its own regard, thereby creating a narrative of its function to relate back to its experiential state. The mind loses its sense of itself, while in the interim it becomes reliant on a fragile conjurement of an admixture of ideals, which leads to more disconnect from its true nature.

"Let's kill the people who taught us to kill."xxi This is based on too many simultaneous ideals, all of which are in no relation to the experiential state of the individual or of general sociality.

The psyche thus requires a superego fissure, through which it begins such leadership, which can conclude in a unity between its regular happenstance, based on the prevalent acceptance of that fissure and disruption. Then again it would be difficult to ascertain that a simple disruption of the psyche would be the creation of a superego, because disruption is not necessarily based on coherence, and the data to which is contained in the disrupting force could be of no consequence to the general happenstance of the psyche.

This embodiment does not translate to the internal superego, despite the embodiment being an internal process. In some sense, every psyche process including perception is internal. It is only to be considered internal when the commencement of the superego is internally found, while this embodiment is only reactionary to the already prevalent external experience.

The reason the psyche responds so considerably to an external superego, defying its entire process of will, is found in the realization that what is hovering is greater and more powerful than its mechanisms, whether material or psychological. This realization has the psyche defy its order of procedure, since the domination is to be considered in all its endowment. Domination itself is so responsive because the psyche experiences a deep dependence on the circumstance of the superego's domination.

Take the case of a father who will be experienced as a persuasive external superego, when there is a realization that the power, sometimes psychological and sometimes material, has the biological system of the child both threatened and as its salvation. The threat of complete domination or promise of salvation is in the way of entering into a communion with the figure, such that they are, in fact, the superego themselves. They have alleviated both the threat and the dependency by making a deal with the domination, so that now they have become the superego, leaving no system that could be dependent or threatened; they are all invested.

Section Three: On the Identification of Being with Consciousness and Its Political Encapsulation

As we have already noted, consciousness is not individualistic, although it merges in based on an assumption; so that if one accepts that integration, they could also assume that the beholders of consciousness, both individuals and being itself, are notions of immortality and therefore deserve to be protected.

In summary, one would not want to experience a death of consciousness within themselves or very well its disruption, for they believe that any form of encapsulation of such consciousness should not be removed from the psyche, and thus may build an entire philosophy around the psyche for protecting the experienced notions of consciousness, though losing its subliminal power.

This supposition is based on two primary existing assumptions. One is the notion that an individual is merged with consciousness experience; for if one already agrees that they are not two distinct entities, consciousness must not be cut from the individual; it is already integrated.

The second supposition, layered upon the first, is that consciousness as an encapsulation is immortal, which is true in a fundamental sense, but also linked to the beholder of such consciousness, who is mortal.

The truth of the matter is that consciousness is an immortal process. It does not require protection for its own sake, for either it is immortal and will flourish whether we intervene or not, or it is mortal and follows its natural course.

The only reason we concern ourselves with the immortality of consciousness is that we assume the beholder is deserving that attribute. They do not want consciousness to die within themselves because they assume that alongside that disruption comes their own degeneration.

Not only have they identified with the substance of consciousness alongside their being, but they have also identified their being alongside the substance of consciousness, so that wherever the consciousness spectrum moves, so does their being. If consciousness dies, so does their being; if it thrives, so does their being.

It is the strongest form of identification, such that at a certain point it is no longer an experience of consciousness but rather a perspective of individual experience, where there is an attempt to control and regulate every movement of consciousness that does not follow its natural wave pattern.

The first supposition is required before the second, for it allows an individual to take possession of consciousness. But not only have they taken possession, they have moved to the second supposition: allowing consciousness, at least in its encapsulated form, to take possession of their being. Thus, they integrate one another, so that the cessation of consciousness is viewed as a cessation of existence.

However, it is not all consciousness that permeates the psyche, one which they protect and associate with their being, but rather only that which they understand, for there are many times when consciousness flows in and out of the psyche without causing disruption, because they do not recognize that conscious substance has entered.

It is only the understood elements of consciousness that are associated with being, and therefore one must rely on an external mechanism to identify what is considered consciousness.

They do not have the internal mechanism to distinguish consciousness from regular psyche processes because not only have they given consciousness a possessive attribute, they have also subsumed existential being as an individualistic experience into that possession, so they cannot fully understand what it is they are possessing.

Thus, they must rely on an external parameter to define what they claim ownership, creating the problematic situation of depending on what is most easily noticed as consciousness by virtue of its accessibility.

This is typically what is most political, for the political parameter is most readily available as a criterion for consciousness. Having decided on a parameter of consciousness, all other possibilities for being, from other parameters of consciousness, are excluded from view, and what remains of perspective is anything related to political origins, because it is the most accessible, most pronounced, and most easily available.

Chapter Six: Environmental Hazards and Perceptual Order

Environmental hazard is one of the most prominent methods that engineers a process of change in relation to perceptual procedure. Because of the embeddedness in which an individual finds themselves in regard to these themes, it is very unlikely that one will find nuance or methodology in relation to its domain. The environmental circumstance will dictate much of this process, in how we have come to categorize personalities by zodiacs, numbered categories, or any other psychological test of the categorical individual. The predictive method made possible, such that if one were in a certain category they are more likely to do such and such, arises because most people are environmentally dictated, and these categories are largely the different methods of perceptual approach and their relation to the rest of the psyche.

Infrastructurally, this is a common theme, where the environmental disruption becomes the quintessential element in how all roads and infrastructure are similar, and then there is a standalone deviation. This hazard is truly a disruption, but because the general sequence must adhere to its internal limitations in dealing with the "diagonal" road, it brings bearing on its character. It becomes fairly difficult to directly interact with a sequential or linear structure because it is made to perform with the cracks and crevices where imagination and creativity can cultivate. Although they are disruptions to the overall theme, by having to deal with both the patterned formula and its disruptions, one finds themselves on uneasy ground. There is no resting reserve on either side, for the crossroad must deal with the diagonal road, and the diagonal will find itself foreign to its embedded circumstance of general crossroads.

The patterned crossroad function is not in itself a problematic formula. It is, in fact, so perfect a perceptual modality that it becomes difficult to distinguish its parameters. However, with enough insight one can approach the patterned formula and notice its perceptual nuance, and they do so by recognizing its subliminal character; its internal diagonal road that is unnoticed by the general sociality. Yet it may be that general sociality is not attuned at that level, such that it requires a complete infrastructural manifestation of a diagonal road in order to perceive its offering of character, though that character was already subliminally embedded in the entire pattern formula, for the pattern must follow from a character and cannot perform itself without an onset of potential, ideation, and performance.

This applies most determinately to the procedure of perception. If one finds themselves in a hazard of differing modalities of perceptual choice, then they may arrive at a fair framework of the complete process, which includes the vantage of both sides. For example, a shadow locale is the cause of perceptual disruption, being that it is not conducive to the actualization of perceptual forms and is also disadvantageous to the interpretation of perceptual form. Since that is the manifestation of that realm, it begins to offer a two-sided notion of perceptuality, providing one both the entire database of how the perceptual process works and the noted dread that comes along with it, all with indications of how to regulate and control it.

However, this is usually not the outcome, and one of two responses is most readily sought: either complete avoidance, whereby, without adherence to that realm, one does not experience a disfigurement of their perceptual process and can continue unabated in whatever modality they have been environmentally engineered to perform, or the actualization of the shadow, whereby the individual becomes the perceptual form that is the shadow. Even if there is no such thing as a perceptual form that can be directly constituted as a shadow being merely the contrast of something else, the psyche has the ability to actualize as if it were the real thing. In this way, instead of having the shadow forbear the entire apparatus of perceptual procedure, one becomes the shadow; for then they do not have the vantage of the prior perceptual state and remain only in this stagnant liminal space which inhabits the offering of one who is participating in a perceptual pathway.

Thus, in this example, the shadow is a natural environmental hazard, which in its initial exposure has the ability to perform the intersection that illuminates the perceptual process and its vulnerabilities and/or possibilities. However, unlike most environmental hazards, the shadow, if actualized as part of one's perceptual modality, incorporates its process and disallows its offering as a vantage to genuine perceptual modality.

In fact, all environmental hazards that are actualized lose their substantiation as modalities that can infer upon the entire perceptual arena. Even the "diagonal" road, if experienced only within its own state, will be the cause of disenfranchisement with the crossroads and will appear as if it were the true sequence of the city. It will not offer its primary characteristic of being "diagonal," since that requires an intersection with crossroads, and thus it will lose the possibility of perspective.

There is the case of an environmental hazard protecting itself from becoming an actualization. In the case of a shadow locale, it is fairly unprotected, since one is inclined to actualize that realm due to the pressing issue of illuminating something that is extremely disruptive to psyche comfortability. Moreover, there is a social manifestation of beings who have actualized that realm and thus offer an agreeable sociality to partake as though they are of the same social strata. Therefore, it becomes pressing as an issue to either actualize or avoid.

In the case of the infrastructural hazard, like the diagonal road, although it is not readily actualized like the shadow, it does not offer a realization of the perceptual apparatus being unearthed because it most closely intersects with the regular sequence. Most would simply assume that it is part of the general sequence and will move readily between realms as if they are the same. The shadow locale performs as it does because it is distinctly of an origin that requires disruption of the regular sequence, whereas the diagonal road is not attempting to disrupt the conceptual experience of the general sequence, only to manifest as an infrastructural distinction.

There is a case where the environmental hazard can perform while avoiding a form of actualization that would disrupt its disrupting character. This occurs when there is a constant change between the perceptual data, such that at one moment it is high regard and at another being limited. Such a locale is not necessarily a shadow, for it simply follows the perceptual manifestations of its terrain. But because of its vulnerability, being at the cusp of perceptual change, it manifests as an automatic experience of disruption. It is almost as if new diagonal roads become part of the infrastructure only to then scale back and repeat the cycle. In such a case, one cannot brush off the new diagonal roads because they are a disruptive force to the current infrastructure, nor can one ignore the scaling-back as manifesting the perceptual sequence that surrounds them.

Thus it becomes a habitat that forces one to constantly take sides without having the ability to actualize at any point. For if they actualize the process of constant change, they are simply following whatever change will occur rather than controlling mobility. It is not a shadow locale because it is not reflecting or contrasting upon a sequence; rather, it is an internal mobility that requires one to acquiesce to its perceptual shifts.

This mobility of an environmental hazard can occur throughout an infrastructure, especially in cases where there is constant fluctuation of sociality at the center of that dependency. Where there is a questionable stature of forward progress within a state, such that the sociality is in constant motion, the entire infrastructural expanse will fluctuate accordingly, in addition to infrastructural deviations that mirror that sociality.

If an individual does not attenuate to this environmental hazard, which is a mobile force, they will degenerate accordingly, as they are in constant fluctuation between perceptual information: at one point assuming continuation where, in fact, it has been removed; then accepting that it is of a lower stature; and then realizing that the perceptual change was itself the cause of a differing structure. In following this cycle on a constant basis, the individual will degenerate in accordance with their perceptual depth, domesticity, and all informational aspects that apply to their conscious bearing and substantiation as a civilized individual. It is as if one entered a ride that degenerated their civilized stature by simply participating. The environment itself is stacked against them, mobilizing any matter that will constantly fluctuate without the ability to attenuate to its minute-by-minute change.

In this case, the only approach to avoid that degeneration is either the conceptual overlay, which, in any conceptual approach, allows one to limit the sociality or perceptual information entering their psyche based on conceptual regulation. However, this conceptual overlay works only if it is interactive with the sociality itself. If it is simply a mathematical layer or some projection of a conceptual approach to the subject, one will be bound to the perceptual outcome because they are not acquiescing to any form of that sociality. As we know, when one avoids the sociality that provides the conceptual process, that sociality reenters as the dominant form of avoidance. Only through direct interaction with the sociality as a manifest reality does one refrain from its actualization since interaction itself suspends that outcome. Likewise, one refrains from its non-actualization by sustaining the interactive basis.

In any realm where there is an unstable perceptual bearing, one finds themselves with only the prospect of interacting with that realm. The other possibility is separation into a domicile reserve. Because a fluctuating realm may have little direct infrastructural attachment, it is possible to find a haven of domesticity that can prove forthcoming so long as there is no interaction with the fluctuating environment. It may even prove advantageous, since the limited perceptual exposure to that fluctuating environment allows for a stream of novelty and nuisance, while, in more static environments, perceptual data may be uniform and thus lack stimulation. However, in the contemporary process, fluctuations are more common, such that we may primarily encounter fluctuating environments in contrast to static ones.

The cause of fluctuation can stem from structural, social, or both causes. When they are structural, they occur in locations on the cusp between marginalized distinctions and broader connections within the infrastructural center. These locations are inherently fluctuating and highly responsive to seasonal, social, and other changing patterns. Typically, they have infrastructural mechanisms in place to regulate these fluctuations; for example, limiting connections in the case of overexposure or heightening them when exposure is low. Although the regulation is usually one-sided, more connection or less, it only responds when contrasted. This is only possible in the directions of south, east, or west, but not North. This is not because of any metaphysical aspect, but rather because the social structure positions North as "on top" and thus beyond direct influence. As a result, every member of the social network, along with the infrastructure that represents it, treats North as a realm apart, not directly influencing or being influenced by the connections that affect the other directions.

There are other aspects of this approach worth discussing, but suffice to say that North does not fluctuate with direct sociality because it avoids exposure. The North acts like a hat to the garment, a reminder of the middle sequence, but with an attempt to outdo or offer a more elevated sentiment. The process is such that the North separates itself by its identity of being "on top," which other directions do not share (as they are defined more by natural exposure than identity). It brings with it a memory of this sociality and attempts to apply something more conciliatory to the ensemble. In this sense, the North is an identity from the outset, and if this identity is removed or neglected, it creates a form of separation, as the rest of the infrastructure has sequestered its exposure. This is why the North has little domesticity: once rooted in identity, there is little incentive to domesticate identity-related themes, which are usually in service to direct exposure.

Social fluctuation occurs when sociality converges in a manner limited by time and sequence. This can have the paradoxical effect of social influence appearing at the beginning, middle, or end of the process. For instance, when a new form of sociality begins to converge, one must engage with it to remain aligned with concurrent sociality. However, if one follows this sociality in real-time, they may find that it has already passed its prime. This is due that such sociality is transient, limited by its time of convergence. If one continues to adhere to this past sociality, they are perpetuating a legacy that no longer exists. This may be acceptable when the realm has become infrastructurally separated, where the formalization of sociality serves merely as a memory, differentiating the parts of that memory. However, in this case, there is still an infrastructural attachment that relies on real-time influence, anchoring the structure to an influence that is no longer relevant.

Realms that successfully detach from their infrastructure still require animation to retain their environment. They achieve this by conceding a certain attachment to facilitate their detachment, using whatever sociality is offered as a platform to distance themselves from that very sociality. Yet, regardless of the outcome of the process, they will still be in association with that sociality, so that in a state of non-convergence, they will be unable to form any definitive structure for their realm, almost like a scattered realm of unavailability. The sociality does expose a form of non-convergence, but it does so to a realm that is already attempting structural detachment, which creates a state of perpetual confusion. Here, both the sociality dictates structural detachment, and the realm uses that same sociality of detachment to distance itself from the attachment. This leaves the final outcome exposed to a kind of unavailability, unable to be either detached or attached. This is why the North is most vulnerable to non-convergence sociality, not as the cause of degeneration, but more as a scattered, disjointed process.

Consider the case of one following the eventual outcome of a convergence of sociality which has now been laid dormant, and to which they may attend in the social realm as if there is a convergence; then, instead, they would be creating an artificial notation of what sociality is when, in fact, it has not been in a state of convergence. In the regular case where there is limited fluctuation, sociality is the standard in which participants maintain its substructure, and at most times it is in a state of convergence. When it does move beyond that convergence, it is a slow, methodical process that has most people participating in its decline and waiting for newfound convergence.

In the case of fluctuating sociality, the time period between non-convergence, convergence, and then non-convergence is at a much faster pace, and therefore it is concerning, fluctuating in all its influence. Because infrastructure is stagnant and complicated as an endeavor, if there is fluctuating sociality, it will be almost impossible to maintain an infrastructure that mirrors that sequence. If the time period of the cycle is lengthy, such as a decade, this allows time for the infrastructure to mirror that process because there is enough dynamical inference to provide details that can manifest in the appearance of infrastructure. However, in the case where such fluctuations occur day by day or week by week, there is no possibility of maintaining an infrastructure that sequences with that, and thereby the fluctuating sociality will constantly change the manifest nature of all infrastructure.

Besides the complication of alignment between infrastructure and sociality that occurs with fluctuating sociality, there is the complication of the attenuation of all dependencies upon that sociality. For one day, there can be a convergence, to which all its dependencies, which might span miles or continents, endeavor to proceed according to that. Then, when the convergence is over, some small town or continent may conclude that there was a continuation of that convergence, and for them, follow a sociality that no longer exists.

In this case of a fluctuating sociality, there is no cusp of that sociality, for every individual is now at the behest of the changing environment and thereby always required to attend to the true nature of that process. Even if no data were available to all people regarding this change of events, it would still occur as long as there is an infrastructural connection that allows for that synchronicity. If, for instance, there is an infrastructure separation, not just a data disruption, then the dependencies are independent of their influential order and must function on their own accord.

One may think that it is the data access that provides the connection between sociality, but rather it is there to determine in what manner there is or is not a form of convergence. The convergence that does occur influences whatever dependencies exist, and those dependents are based on the infrastructural attachment and the layered sociality above that. It is not because of the data access or the knowledge of occurrences, but the subliminal nuances between social beings that proceed in accordance and pass faster than any data can be received. The exact process by which this occurs requires diligent study, but suffice it to say that it is not the data access and its layered material that provides any sort of social or infrastructural manifestation, but only as though it is a library to understand the existential occurrences. It has no existential bearing of its own accord but can influence as any library can influence individuals toward an existential occurrence. If air travel were dismantled overnight, there would be a dramatic change in infrastructure status, prompting a redesign of all influences and exposures.

The sociality that converges at the center is only required to be an exposure toward its dependencies. If the dependencies are in a state of availability, they will experience that convergence. If they are in a state of independent posturing or assuming alternative socialities of a previous or simulated moment, they will be unavailable to such convergence but disruptive in utilizing one form of sociality to exaggerate their independence.

In the opposite case, if there is a failure of convergence at the center, then the subsidiaries may presume a convergence or some form of posturing to thus rely on a dead-end state of sociality which has its consequences. Alternatively, they can agree to a lack of convergence, which will be a form of influence yet complicated to recognize. Even when sociality has broken down as a form of convergence, there is still a diminutive form of sociality alongside non-convergence: it is a convergence of non-convergent material, which becomes the influential measure, much like in how the winter season bears an accepted non-convergence at the center, to which all substrates experience its non-convergence elements, allowing for the domesticated holiday experience.

The influential call of non-convergence is the compartmentalization required at whatever state the subsidiary remains, to which they can then rearticulate their internal domain. They are still reliant upon their perceptual data of non-convergence, almost like a manager who demands a recounting of systems. Following the non-convergence elements to their center origin would be disruptive, since there is no conversion to non-convergence, despite there having been a convergence of it. Moreover, if there is no internal articulation, one either postures their own formation of what constitutes that sociality or becomes actualized to the compartmentalization of the environment they are part of, all instead of articulating as though there is no convergence. It is not a state of convergence for that domesticated and seasonal realm but rather as a state of non-convergence at every level, to which one is allowed to attend the domesticated realm and rely on the center influence while still requiring non-convergence in the domesticated realm itself. This is commonly misunderstood, and rather has the household actualize themselves in these realms, which is disruptive to many systems.

Part 2: Representations and Reflection

Chapter One: Architecture of Representation

Section One: Notation & Default: Foundations of Personhood

Personhood in its entirety is ambiguous and only the chosen representations at any interval either to itself or to others will be the variety that can be utilized for interaction. We can imagine the egoless person without the defense of selfhood or its propagation, nor the expression, for there is no seat for personhood to actualize. Happenings occur but without deliberations of personhood, external perspectives are attended perpendicular to this person but as others' peculiar projection for representation. The notation in psychology is that there is always an former or immature ego which succeeds the moment for any experience of the psyche. If we were to dispel the current ego, another ego will take its place, just as if we were to lose representation, another will take its place. It is only the matter of sophistication of the representative in its incorporation with the most current material which successfully reflects the present happenings in expression form.

When a family member is perceived without a certain notation, a default notation will take its place. When the default representation ascends from a distant part of the wholeness of person or to put it succinctly, from an infantile aspect of themselves, they immediately take upon that representation and interact with them in accordance. The default notation is going to be the last place of residence for a representation. For it to revert to an infantile measure would mean that the current representation has been constructed without any background of preceding representation which are similar to confirm a slow sign of mature progress. The current representation has taken effect by conscious activity which placed it there and not developed from continuous conversation. To place a representation upon any individual can immediately have its effect, although, when depreciated there may be no prior representation to fall back upon. The enterprise of placing the representation was enacted so as to engage in accordance with an individual.

However, when that representation is not forthcoming, the entire individual becomes involved in conjuring a new one. It may dig into a far deeper past to find idiomatic material that would make for a relatable representation for further engagement. We cannot dismantle the entirety of the relationship because the representation has offered major themes of personhood to the psyche. Those themes can be based on infantile measures, and so we have the encroachment on infantile parts for further representations. We can identify a link from the current representation to the infantile aspect, which followed an arduous journey of significant shifts until we reach the current one. However, the psyche does not pick up on all those junctures of change for certain reasons. This can usually be attributed to a lapse of awareness at those junctures, so that the default ground that was consciously brought to animation may be found in infantile stages. The later junctures are prominent in providing the current representation; however, they fall short of being a revisionary measure because they are not enjoined in the conscious system.

Not all psyche material is to be represented, only that which is deserving to be formulated for production, which we term expression. There are two criteria of the psyche deemed undeserving, either for their antagonistic nature in the external forum or for their lack of primacy regarding the true objectives of personhood. The existential experience will be antagonistic, even as it makes up an important part of the psyche, yet it is also not primary because it is always in how we perform despite the existential nature. Many cases of mental deterioration are representations of existential portions of personhood and are not taken very well by social environments. Instead of having a primary casing despite those realities, they have chosen residence in those departments of the psyche. The social environment is not appreciative toward such representations because it does not seek to observe other social kinds as merely in existential disarray, for it assumes wholeness of personhood when perceiving a representation. Thus, it concludes that personhood is merely existential chaos, and those primary aspects which are sought become diminished.

There is a spectrum of representation, the extremes of which are respectively absolute fabrication or expression that seems not to revere the representation. Anything less than that will be ordained regression toward an inevitable representation agreed upon by the psyche.xxii For instance, if clothing is not intended to represent, then the representation is compelled to be either the "non-intention" intention or the "clothed man," as opposed to vulgar nakedness. Still, there may be subtle representations that may be elusive to selfhood but are nonetheless enacted by the psyche. These may not be keenly present in the conscious arena but are representations that underlie subconscious deliberations.

A uniform is classical clothing that provides a transparent viewing of the individual through the representation. This is also the representation that the individual experiences about themselves, which provides an extra layer of trust for sociality. The transparency allows a free-moving society not to require excessive judgment and concern in dealing with important social roles. This is the reason that uniforms are most adhered to in government systems, as they also represent the unity of the institution in their representation of society. There are no individuals representing the government; indeed, government is a mere representation of society, which is reflected in the uniform. The interaction with those individuals is usually from the standpoint of their representation. An underdeveloped government would find an individualistic expression for its service members, which creates gaps in the overall representation, or, more intuitively, represents its overall inconsistency.

The fabrication of a representation is the conscious attention to a specific aspect that does not narrate the entire picture. For example, when one dons a government uniform, the attire signifies their affiliation with the state, suggesting a comprehensive representation. However, this uniform only encapsulates a fraction of their personhood. By allowing this governmental aspect to overshadow the broader scope of their personhood, they perpetrate a significant misrepresentation based on a small semblance of truth. Moreover, the government official is not wholly encompassed by the role symbolized by the uniform, either in the nuanced responsibilities of their position, which, in their intricate details, require a personal perspective that cannot derive from a systematic structure, or in the complicated dimensions of their personal identity that cannot be tied to a broad generalization. Nonetheless, a substantial part of their identity is dedicated to the intricacies of their official role.

The one who is egoless, at least for the moment, should not be noticed as a representation by the social environment. Others are not willing to adhere to their own representation while also having another social being represent the notion that personhood is a non-representative perspective of existence. Indeed, the empathetic stance will be to take upon themselves the altruistic notion of adding a representation to those lacking one. Almost as a generosity to the underdeveloped, they grant a development to them without admittance to their personhood, which happens to lack the ability, so as to entertain their attention sphere to be filled without any deviants. This cannot be done to every passerby because we are unable to match the entire sphere of influence, and we consider a form of generosity to be given to those who assume a role or are a material vessel. The material vessel pertains to those who promise existential depth and relational embodiment, and it is these two that are in conflict for the given representation.

Existential depth pertains to those who objectively contain such, while relational embodiment refers to those who mirror our biological experience. The stranger is not in relational embodiment by the default strangeness, but those strangers in political or social representation will promise existential depth and embodied relationality. The relationality is provided because the majority has taken interest, in which the individual becomes a member of the social class they are in relation to and thus an able representation. Therefore, the majority's representations allow the embodiment of their depth to be integrated into the citizens' personhood but do not offer a bargain on existential depth or even individuation.

This pertains to the specific person and their adeptness in this domain. We often find that these social representations, although offering embodiment and thus a provision despite depth, will prove disappointing for extracting material. We may wonder about the development of the majority, if they merely contain a populace that is in representation mode to the majority, with the inevitable perpetual emptiness: the group is the people, which are the group. This is the plague of the majority's representations, as the majority does not embody depth but only enough for an experience to be meted out for each individual. We could define the experience of a single individual within that setting as deriving enough vitality to continue their charade while not enough to incentivize a personal journey.

Those in a position of recognition do not follow the details to that accessible growth but enjoy the surface, as one would the fine cuisine at a social event. The intuitive understanding of those within that representation is that the surface material is never the primary access to the depth that is available. The luxurious class would never speak or even think of the luxury, since this would cause the representation to offer slight shavings of availability to the service of that luxury, namely, existential personhood. The momentary lapse to enjoin in a specificity of the elaborate themes and amenities becomes the habitat for assuming that the representation is its end, rather than an exemplified aspect of personhood meant to stimulate conceptual mystification. This would be the perspective of the child who perceives the glistening glow and assumes it is a point of convergence, while the adult knows it is only an illumination to follow its representation, the true convergence being personal awareness. We may presuppose that representations are surface-like as a sweeping criticism, but upon further notice, the nature of the surface-like aspects cultivates the representations to be available at an existential depth.

The majority's representations are not lacking existential depth; it is the majority's journey to such that is limited. Without that expressed representation, they would be unable to become the majority's representation. The majority cannot continuously project a representation if it is not agreed upon and cultivated by the individual. The nature of representations is that they need a hosting source within absolute personhood. For a majority to take up a representation requires the hosting services of its members. These individuals will experience a certain existential depth that is immediately absorbed by that representation. That existential depth must be tamed, enough to vitalize and grant a living movement to the representation, but short of having them depart from it.

The individuals who balance these two sides are the greatest asset to any group or majority. Those who slowly move away from the representation are the most despised, for influencing the group while also towing the line toward drastic movements that cause disarray among the rest. Most individuals are not privy to the handling of their own personhood, and when there are drastic movements in the representation to which they adhere, they become disoriented and begin to enter their own existential journey. Different from the balanced individuals, these proponents are interested in removing the troubling experience and will disrupt the group or the social environment to achieve that objective.

The details of that existential depth may not be known by the individual of a group's representation. This personal depth is only attuned to that which has the ability to partake in the existential growth of the majority. The aspects of these individuals' relationships are a fine offering to the representation, while conceptual formulas of any kind will not prove advantageous to the group. A representation cannot perform the task of granting mental fabrications the light of day when they cannot take place in the sociality from which they are born. If the personal aspects cannot be socialized in a large forum, they will be unable to be embedded in the representation. This is why the group will not find favor in conceptual developments, for they are immediately antagonistic to the necessities of the representation. When there is a recommendation for conceptual outreach, it is only to perform the menial task of having individuals existentially attach to the representation.

We could find aspects of sociality if we follow conceptual progress, yet it will be distributed through metaphors and external representations that could not be foreseen. As well, the conceptual perspective will take new forms according to a preordained social dynamic. We could even predict the manner of approach to conceptual ideas according to the sociality that we observe. Plato's Republic is a prime example, it is used to represent according to the sociality of a given time, one reader assuming it to be the description of an absolute state to be envisioned, while another recognizes its ironic undertone of "Tell me, Glaucon!" A representation uses conceptual complexities for its social advantage, and its core dynamism is the manner of sociality itself.xxiii

For instance, a scientist within a troubled social paradigm, or one who enters into the domain of representation, or any other existential detail, can disrupt, propel, or extinguish their scientific work. The threatening or promising nature of that science exists only in its representation for individuals and societies that will either enjoy or fear it. For example, medical progress may prolong lives that do not want to live; or anxiety may be assumed to be a symptom of personal unruliness, a societal symptom of decline represented in the individual, a heightened awareness of a developing consciousness, or a symptom of a decline in consciousness.

Returning to the projection of a representation onto individuals or groups that lack one: as we attempt to fulfill the generosity quota beyond its maximum, we allow it to represent a mass, which causes the projection to be over-general and disillusioned, either taking on a limited perspective of existence (as will be discussed, e.g., "people of this kind of city") or distracting toward elemental subjects that offer material both substantial and related to one's biological center.

"Center" refers to those in proximity to their gene pool, absolute biological or in relation to the biological existence. Even so, the gene pool must be distinguished from including all of its intimate strains, as it would distract from relations in its developmental future. Just as members within one's genial lineage are conceptually removed from their biological status, so too are those in relational proximity or simply strangers, to be incorporated or removed as is good for central personhood.

The same applies to those who do not have a representation of themselves. In their perspective of others, they perceive them as objects without continuity or consistency. They project their non-representation upon others, forcing the appearance that all humans are itemized confusions. When this becomes impossible, on the occasion that the representation is clearly a perception of the multiplicity of the external realm, they must project the most general or simplistic overview to allow themselves to brush past it. Just as personhood will contain general representations for its ability to function, with disintegration or absolute confusion, those mediocre representations become the points of projection that allow one to continue avoiding the affair of life. They will resort to major categories such as good or evil, happy or sad, rich or poor. Having the entire population thrown into these very extensive categories, they assume them with representations that are inept for anything but the avoidance of complete disintegration. If half are evil and the other good, the evil are to be avoided without any further deliberation, and the good are to be assumed at par and disgraceful for further questioning. If one is sad, they need happiness; while one who is happy has found all that is needed, without any nuance to the notions of "sadness" and "happiness."

Representation is an actualization of an established persona, for the psyche is vast and must be compacted into a small narrative structure suited to this time and space. As the moment continues alongside space, that representation cannot remain a composite of this new form of personhood; it is deserving of a new composite. Since the first representation was streamlined to fit a small capsule, it would be that same variety that could work for another layout of composite materials; just as a poetic line may be appropriate for a variety of occasions.

However, since we know that the composite materials are different, using the same representation would call the psyche to order, to repeat, in place, the state it occupied in a previous time and setting. As when a poetic line serves as the groundwork for an insightful change, the attempt to reuse that same line in the next stage would demand the psyche remain consistent with the original material that first brought the verse into being. The psyche does so because it follows the chain of thought that revisits the initial state of affairs to extract that verse; it would not have found it otherwise, given its original impact.

A representation works in the same fashion, worthwhile only in its manifest moment, and is deserving of a unique composition that cannot be reoffered in any other context. For instance, to perform a setting that adequately describes an experience, one would arrange the environment as a representation of such. Even if the natural state of affairs does not pause to perform its best moments, the representation will do so, in order to adequately convey the situation that an ordinary moment could not suffice to express.

Clothing offers a fitting example: the natural state of movement is man in nakedness, but since such abundant information would distract from interaction, one wears clothing to represent oneself within the short attention span of the social environment. Were the occasion such that one's attention could be detailed without judgment or conclusion, then nakedness might be appropriate, as in art performance. The body would then serve either as a representation of the human form, its feminine and masculine features, or as personhood displayed in rawness, with an availability of attention that would not conclude with abominating properties, as is the case with a normally naked person.

Section Three: Center Gravity and Representation

To the degree of existential attachment is the capacity to represent material in accordance to the center gravity of one's psyche. When existential attachment is minimal then the representing material is going to be further from center gravity. The familial member is existentially attached, so that their representation is near the center gravity. The stranger is not existentially attached, such that their representation is not near center gravity. Despite the representation that imbues a stranger being all that is unknown, quite vaster than what is known, it is not a representation that interacts with the core components of the psyche. This is why the unknown is only fearful when there is a lack of fulfillment in what is already known.

When the interactive components of the psyche are appropriately handled in both external form and internal dialogue, the notion of a fearful unknown will not disquiet the psyche. That is, the stranger becomes more relevant as a representation when they elicit certain sensibility to the gaps in one's center gravity. Although called strangeness, it is really the neglected components of the familial and/or internal space.

One can form an existential attachment that brings a representation close to gravitational center, though it will always reflect former representations. For example, any friend will be a representation of one's familial body, and similarly, intimate interactions will mirror that same familial body. When intimacy reaches a level of existential attachment, it becomes a representation of one's childhood familial body. Both forms of attachment serve each other, and removing one representation would cause harm to both.

The same paradigm can be applied to structural consciousness. The existential attachment of the collective consciousness, which can only be at a single geographical location, will consist of representations which are near to the center gravity of that attachment. While what is not existentially attached to collective consciousness will contain representations that are far from center gravity. This would mean that within a non-existentially attached location, will produce a representation that is not applicable to collective consciousness and thus immaterial to the culminating populace. The representations are made possible by the reception of the center of gravity. Depending on its distance from the existential attachment, it will manifest in an inconsequential manner, similar to how a stranger provides a representation for an individual that does not offer significant insight for the psyche. Overly general and systematic representations are responses from the stranger, due to their distance from the center of gravity. However, when one forms an existential attachment to a stranger, they enter into a familial domain, causing their representations to become relevant to personhood.

The physical manifestation is the baseline for representation in any aspect, but the difference lies in the departure from physical representation to existential reality. They both occur together. That is, a cup represents both a drinking object and the experience of the drinking object in its provision for liquid. Anybody who has drunk from a cup will be both a part of the existential representation, with the cup being a representation of liquid ingestion, and a thoughtful purview of the cup in its representation for liquid.

To note some of the differences: the physical experience of drinking from a cup contains material of hand motions, body interaction, sipping, weight, and structure, while the existential perspective will concern liquid and its need for molds, as well as the separation of liquid and ingestion. We could study the fingertip sensations of drinking and find dominance of the finger over the arm, which in turn treats the liquid with sensitivity, whereas food, which uses more the overall hand and the subsequent arm, is treated with more roughness. This can be considered a research topic, but I would not have stumbled upon it had I not drunk from a cup. In fact, for the existential perspective, I required little imagination of the process of drinking and rather enjoyed an abstract realm for those ideas. When I sought to find the physical material of that representation, I had to repeat the imaginative process of drinking until I identified areas of representation.

We could claim that if the imagination is a realm in which all physical representations can manifest, that is true, but only when the physical experience has followed to the degree that the imagination becomes integral. If we ask a child what it means to be a king, they might say "to be strong," which the mature person will understand in their imagination with a more accurate picture. The imagination has been developed through interactions in the physical realm, which coincide with royal aspects that have been understood through the test of time. The imagination that could conjure the most accurate existential experience of being a genuine king has been entertaining the notion through their physical intersections with the subject, which eventually paralleled. They may have imitated the role or followed royalty to identify aspects that could restructure their imagination to be aligned.

To provide the opposite extreme of such: the experience of royalty in a strict monarchy is only going to be a physical experience for those in that royal structure. In fact, it is specifically the king who will be able to existentially experience royalty in its finest and truest sense. Therefore, only a single person will be able to interact with the representation in an affective way. Everyone else is systematically divorced from the existential experience and will only be able to afford such a sense through a representation deprived of a formidable existential experience.

In both scenarios we have provided, certain aspects naturally occur in both for most of civilization. A certain trade, such as that of a doctor, can only be an existential representation if one is truly a doctor. While the doctor will never be able to partake in the existential representation of nursing, the reason I say "never" is because they have already obtained another representation, which exhausts their existential experience in the adjacent field. However, the nurse can partake in the existential experience of doctoring because doctoring includes nursing, while nursing does not include doctoring. The clientele is always at the behest of the medical procedure, in which nursing provides an intermediary. Thus, if we do not have clientele for medical procedures, there cannot be doctoring. Medical procedures cannot be followed without an intermediary role, which involves the doctor in direct dynamic with the patient.

That is not to say that the philosopher partakes in all trades, roles, and subjects, as it follows the theory above those things. Instead, it is the philosopher's inability to existentially experience anything beneath it that affords such an ability. The philosopher contains the representations, as for instance royalty, by the very outlook of its study. The philosopher may know the concept of royalty in finer detail than any king has entertained. However, the philosopher has never experienced being king and will never have the notion of royal representation in their living life. Therefore, the philosopher does not really know anything at all, just as the doctor does not know anything about the patient. The doctor knows the human body, of which the patient is a participant, but does not know the existential nature of the patient mode in which they are doctoring upon.

Details obtained during an existential experience will be an embodiment of that representation. The intellectual material that is obtained by the king will be aspects which the philosopher will never obtain. The elite of society will be existentially partaking in the representation of being elite, and for that, they embody those details. The sub-elite of society will likewise be existentially partaking in the representation of their sub-elite status. The sub-elite will be noted in their representation of being sub-elite in contrast to the elite, but will not be removed from the system of status. Because of this experience, the sub-elite will always be tempted to divorce from the system and enact a composite structure in which they are elites, as would Virgil says, to be the master of a lizard. Indeed, because of their dependence on the system that they reside in, they will enact the sub-elite representation wherever they view themselves.xxiv

Individuation within development will be receptive according to the parameters and structures in place, so that we could argue most of civilized progress reflects the advancement of the civilized order rather than distinct individual segmentations. We do, however, allude to individuation, which, though as receptive as any other element within the tapestry of culture's feminine attributes, has at times exemplified itself to a magnitude that would not be possible otherwise. Still, this noteworthy individuation remains an exemplary manifestation of the civilized order, only that he or she has followed the points of necessity with such capacity that no other outcome would have been possible. It is important to note that the civilized order arises from the amelioration of individuals; rather than being an individuation, it is a system greater than the sum of its parts.

The potency of representation which catches the eye of the civilized order can be grouped into two categories. One, is the underlying complexity which makes itself known through representation but by no means is presuming that representation. This does include the mental awareness that existential or conscious development is inextricably linked to personal representation, even as the social sphere has not attended to it. Therefore, absolute development would include one's attention to the representation, but differs from the second category by the intention towards further development and not to the receptivity of its substance.

While the receptivity will be noticed, it will be research data for the developmental platform. When the receptivity is aligned with personal representations of one's development, it only matches what is already known. The inevitable deviation in the receptive realm would not be an alarm to the development platform. The social sphere will usually not align with the deserving representation, for it must account for much complexity and moving parts that we can only gain a whim of reasonability for under-or-over evaluation. The receptive data can denote a specific area of representation, even as the entirety of development lies in the shadow.

When that social receptivity is followed to the real representation, then only a specific area of development will continue and the rest will be forgotten. We can perceive the receptive data as an objective form of study which should not contain practical ramifications. The attention sphere to the components reaching the receptive platform and to those which are not, should be equal.

We could argue that what is receptive is worthwhile, while the others are not. However, we cannot understand the ultimate receptivity which is deserving of each individual, nor can the social market follow, thus requiring us to assume a personal representation that includes the entirety of the developmental platform. The social market moves fairly quickly to not be considered an establishment of true representation.

Keeping in mind that individual representation is a developmental stage from infantile to maturity, which surely does not directly interact with the market. Parental attention will not be to have the child represent the social market because they do not have a personal representation to contrast it. They would be lost to the social market and whatever is personal to them does not have a representation which oversees its developments. The personal aspects will inevitably be enlarged since there is an individual underneath the representation, however, they are infantile perspectives which become troubling in the social market. Although it would seem they represent the social market, according to the infantile traits would be in how they manifest that representation. In reality, whatever their infantile traits are, they are still embodying the true market, contrary to their critics, it is only the question of how they attach to the representation.

We could view the mode of parenting as to imbue the child with a personal representation even though the social market is not aligned with them. If the social market somehow finds and presents a representation to the individual, parenting would disengage the potency of the market so that individual representation can take effect.

Another counter measure to the social market's presentation is to have the individual interact with the substance of the representation against the experience of it. The substance would be the personal elements that are brought to bear, which is only the humanizing content which is relatable like any other material. This must be done against the representation, as it continuously seeks to provide a vantage view of the overall picture. The parental figure can follow that representation for important distribution to the immature mind, which will serve as a mediation to the potency of the social market. However, the parental mind must not view the representation as a true analysis but rather an objective point of view that should or should not be detailed for further study.

There is also a logical inconsistency with this argument, for we would agree that individual development is the core function of society. How could individual progress be made if the present market and its representation towards individuals specifically discounts individual-progress that is outside its receptivity? If the market had a voice it would say, "whatever the development occurring in the private realm should be discounted because it is not receptive to the present moment." If such were followed in exactness, society would not be able to function. All individual progress will be superseded to the market's receptivity, to which the market is only an amelioration of individual development. Thus, disparity between personal and social representation is a core function of society and not a fault.

When the disparity is too large then we have a social market that represents itself against personal development. This may seem impossible, as the social market follows the amelioration of individuals for this very reason. The reason it does so is that individual development is continually represented according to the present market's receptivity. This indicates a problematic function at the individual level, where strides toward individuation are made only to conform to social representation rather than to construct one's own.

A recurring narrative arc in the tradition of civilization is individuation presented in contrast to the market's representation. An ensuing dilemma occurs until the choice is made to revert back to individuation. However, the generalization of this narrative structure is worthwhile for an infantile system of thought which supports the individual over the market, especially under the parenting structure. In maturity, however, this narrative presumes to somehow depict that they are not linked, and it becomes a simplistic choice between good and evil. As mature-minded, we can follow the same narrative structure to identify the conclusion as inconclusive and thus follow the complexity throughout the story. The arc will be noted by junctures which require that the market's representation should be noted in its objective form, while individuation should be followed in its depth.

The arc is produced when the market begins to become subjective, or when individuation has not been followed to its sufficient depth. In fact, we could take the path of individuation to sufficient depth, and this would be considered a fulfillment of the market. Within the depth of individuation are personal connections to the market or parental representations which require attention. The same can be said if the market is tended alone, keeping the material as objective as possible. Eventually, the objective research will make its way into one's personal realm and will affect and produce within individuation. So the character who follows the market against individuation is only failing because of the subjective interpretation of the market, which is represented by the loss of their individuation.

The loss of individuation is not the problem, as all science is made of that fabric, but rather the subjective interpretation. Rarely is the narrative structured in which individuation is followed against the market, because it would be easier to produce shallow individuation even though there is a natural contrast of an objective market which necessitates tending. This does not respect the reality of the market, as if it were built separate from the sociality to which it connects. The outcome for a successful narrative would be the continuation of both sides of the spectrum, which is complex to write and depict, and even more so to follow.

Therefore, the social market continues its representation as if no change is occurring, to which each individual will reluctantly agree, all the while the individual progress is not being heard, neither by the individual nor by the social market. The primary reason this occurs is because individuals do not understand the pathway to personal representation, which is different from social receptivity, nor do they believe that it is a necessity for a flourishing society, e.g., the philosopher and the king.

Another argument can be made about the inevitable misfortune of the disengagement of social receptivity. This too can be mitigated by not ignoring the receptive realm but recognizing that the market's attention does not account for the reality of the universe. Moreover, the personal representation needs to be borrowed from the social sphere of influence, which will attend to the details of society. We cannot actualize the personal realm without following the civilized order and its meccas for those associations. The idea is that the imaginative realm will suffice to include oneself into the strata of people that are the pillars of civilization. As such, to not enter into a fantasy, one must attend to those domains and existentially partake so that it is a true manifestation of affairs. Then one can discount the conflict of the social sphere in its lack of receptivity by recognizing the complex structure of sociality as not being available to the authenticity of reality.

Section Five: Vitalizing Representations

Existential attachment becomes the habitat for representation, while non-existential attachment is not privy to natural representation. A high mode of representation is in the epicenter of civilization which will cause the participating members to follow elements of representation in most of their interactions. Communal consciousness has relegated a sensibility to enlarge what would be objects of no interest to assume the role of representing essentials of that consciousness. This communal process has recruited the environment to personalize itself in a manner that will offer face and speech to its content.

This will only highlight the most interactive components of that consciousness. Certain aspects will be presumed to be a part of that representation even as they are simply interactive material of the universe. The representation only becomes a vitalizing force when communal consciousness has chosen its role. This continuously changes, so that what was yesterday's representations will be today's mediocre piece of nature, or worse, its shadow.

The populace may follow what has already been removed from the equation, either out of nostalgic sentiment or, worse, under the assumption that it is interacting with a stimulating force, whereas it is only their projection upon it. We can acknowledge this when there is mental excess to administer sentimental relevance to whatever is the interaction. By the fact that the individual or group must utilize much of their mental metabolism for the interaction demonstrates that the vitalization of the object is not consistent.

When one approaches a vitalizing representation of communal consciousness, they do not require a conceptual overlay or physical exertion; it makes itself to be an incorporating element of universality. This is why biases and self-denial are so troublesome of a trait, owing to the sharp association of a conceptual thrust towards relics of representation in the assumption of true consciousness. The conceptual realm does not need to explain true representations, nor does the physical access become complicated, confusing, or limited. These are aspects of lost representation, as they are elements of a conceptual or physical restriction which denotes a requirement to personify what is actually not animated.

Ironically enough, the same element of true representation can be interacted from either a real incorporation or through individual projection. To wonder why a person would need to project personhood to something that is already vitalizing is due to their lack of understanding or availability to something that already represents for their benefit. They are so close to the object of interest that they sabotage the experience by placing their own conceptual biases to invigorate a process. What is occurring is that something which was already animated is now becoming diminished to non-substantive representation, which then has the individual personify it for the experience of representation.

This is also the occurrence of following the representation with too much attention, that has the individual lose their subjective stance of interaction and instead incorporates the object of interest to be a part of their personhood, thus projecting their own sentiment upon what is considered themselves, instead of the interaction with a revitalizing force of nature without such requirements.

The experience of assuming an interactive component to be stimulating itself, when it is merely a personification, is the cause of personhood decline. Although one could follow the representing elements of any aspect because it does not embellish the dynamism of its representation, what happens is that the aspect is manipulated to seem as if it were vitalized. The only way this is possible is if an individual utilizes their own vitality to systemize the aspect of interest.

First, they must incorporate the aspect into their personhood, as part of their vitality, to then consider it an external substance of interaction. All the while, the interaction is an internal occurrence, with the external substance partaking at no interval. The incorporation is an internalization of an assumed diagram of the external substance; the personification is vitalizing one's own system, and finally, the extraction of the substance to be assumed as an outside element is done only in a contrived form. The externalization is only done so that it would seem like an external process, even though the conceptual movements are internal from beginning to end.

Chapter Two: Representations and Infrastructure

Due to the overwhelming effect that representations have in taking a predominant effect which gets closer to a central theme, the further one goes from that central theme, so does the representations. In effect, the representation that is further from the center might seek to be a performative experience which does not seem to distance itself, because the only sense of relevance for them is to pinpoint a representation that represents the representation. When one attempts to place a representation upon the central theme without affording the distance and disparity between them, what occurs is either they lose relevance in social recognition, or they do so with an subconscious theme of only representing a representation.

We notice this architecturally, for the representation of the center will be in the central locale, and the attempt at being distant from that central locale while still providing a nuanced representation of a central theme would go unnoticed. It would appear to follow a different order of themes where, instead of becoming a representation, it is rather a projection of ideas and expressions that are only afforded recognition according to a representational theme. Even in the process of corporate structures, what is outside of the central theme will only be a representation of what it would be like to be a corporation that represents the central theme. When the corporation attempts to follow its own authority and represent toward the central theme, it does so with the subconscious theme of merely being a representation of the representation. It does not have the ability to proceed and create something new in the representational sphere because it is subservient and dependent upon the reflection and experience of the corporeal entity which does represent the central locale.

It might be easier to define this process as individuals, systems, and infrastructures that merely play the game of imitation because they are deficient in the ability to do more, to be more creative, to be more artistic, to be more ingenious in their approach. However, it is not within their ability, as there is a level of distance and disparity providing only the opportunity to perform the most perfected representation of the representation rather than be a representation themselves. At the behest of reaching that level of perfection, the only possibility for an individual, for a group, for a system, is to partake in the central locale itself to thus become available for the ability to represent the central theme.

However, we are not being fair to the full process. We may have alluded to a representation of a central theme and then the possibility of representing the representation. Indeed, this may be true, but the full scope is based on many layers with multitudes that enjoin in this process. It is possible for a representation to be many times removed from the true representation, but as it gets more removed, its potential and possibility diminish. For the highest level is simply to be a perfected form of representation that is still wholly removed from the equation of the central theme.

The defining factor that affords a space or an individual their degree of possibility, -all in the chain of representations, -is primarily a structural factor. The structural separation, which also includes the social agreement and permeation of such separation, has the full effect of this memory and ability for one to represent the central theme or only to represent the representation. We have discussed in other works a further inquiry into the process and degree of separation and the composite of the structural environment as well as its interaction with consciousness. To remain true to the topic, we suffice to agree that there is a structural factor that defines and creates the separation of space and sociality. We will call these borders, and upon the departure from the first border, one is only able to be a representation of a representation. Upon separation from the second border, one is only able to be a representation of a representation of a representation. The third border: four times removed, and the fourth: five times removed. Once we leave the third border and especially the fourth, it is usually outside the political system and rather takes a global aspect.

The peak of second-tier representation is that it understands the wholeness of first-tier representation so much so that it provides a nuanced perspective and a differing vantage point that erases a certain self-awareness of the first-tier representation. It proves indispensable to provide a perspective on the first-tier representation which even the subjective experience of the first-tier representation would have no effect. This requires a deep analysis of the structure of the representation to understand its vulnerabilities, its advantages, its effects, and with all this, to encompass every articulation of that representation which differs from it so that it could offer a new vantage upon the situation. If all this understanding colludes together but is performed as a direct critique or a direct form of platitude towards the first-tier representation, then it would lose its effect. This is because, although it does have the information to direct one to a deeper analysis of the first-tier representation, it does not provide a platform of its own realm to perform the representation. It israther a conceptual overdrive that demands attention but does not give the opportunity to enter and explore that realm as a nuanced and distinctive place of experience.

We would notice that the most competent secondary representations are a complex array of deep understanding which are not expected and expressed, almost subliminal in the first-tier experience, as well as the performative gesture of being separate, distinct, and almost unnoticeable as being a conversation of anything other than itself. These two traits are the characteristics that reach a perfect form of representation for the second-tier level.

We would find an array of localities in the second-tier level, an array of individuals and groups who will encompass a high degree of analysis, of understanding in the first-tier representation, but only becoming limited and narrow because they do not perform the gesture of being a distinctive locality that appears as its own without any noticeable connection to the first tier. This is a complicated feat because it is for the ability of this perfected form to provide the depth of a representation in the first tier which cannot be performed alongside the first tier, becoming indispensable as a performative structure, as well as never indicating, at least not to the commonality of the social sphere, that it is doing just that. Instead, it needs to be experienced, especially for infantile stages of development, as a true locale of its own merit.

We find the alternative in the second-tier locale as well, where localities, individuals, groups, and infrastructures all perform the virtue of proclaiming their independence and distinctiveness as proposed environments. They do so without any nuanced perspective on the first tier; without any degree of indispensability towards being a provision of anything worthwhile in the first tier. All the while, the second-tier representation will only be a performative structure of any regard to the social system if it follows the details of the first tier. Thus, even without acknowledgment, these systems will enjoin to follow as a response to the first tier, even in their proclamation. With the presumption that they are independent entities, they do not have the ability or capability to follow any degree of nuance or change for gaining a vantage point of the first tier. They simply follow the easiest route that will make them viable options to be relevant in their localized sphere but will not be a new vantage point to offer any new information on the subject. They are essentially borrowing from the first tier for their vitality but do not pay back by providing a nuanced and differentiating perspective.

In some cases, they may seek to enter the third tier, even as their structural environment is second-tier, so that it automatically becomes a coveted space to provide anyone's perspective on the very environment that is surrounding them. Indeed, entering into a third-tier representation does have the advantage of providing something that is not amicable in a second-tier environment, similar to the occasion of providing a second-tier representation within the locality of the first tier. Yet, because the surrounding environment is penetrable to their habitat with so much influence at every turn, the ability to retain and maintain a differing tier from the environment comes either as an extreme, in which it is cut off from any lineage to other social manifestations, or simply acts in any manner of being a third tier while repurposing itself as a second tier.

We notice this with religious entities within the central locale, which in any effect proves to be simply a repurposing of a first-tier representation that only has the illusion of being second-tier and nuanced, separated from the first-tier environment. The same can be said with a second-tier environment, in which to become a third tier would only be a repurposing of a second tier. However, if this repurposing occurs on the occasion of providing a nuanced perspective on the second tier in which it proves indispensable to provide a data point to the second tier that might not have the ability within a true second tier, then it becomes distinguishable not as a performance of a third tier but as a second tier that becomes purposeful as a self-reflection.

For instance, in the case of religion in a first-tier environment, it can become a purposeful vantage point in understanding the process of the first tier, even as it remains a first tier and appears as being in a second tier. This makes the environment structured as a first tier, while within its domain, it is simply a self-critique and self-analysis of its internal system. It is not an external performance to another criterion but rather a display of selfhood that chooses to watch its distinctive parts.

A representational structure has the ability to form not only its representational attributes according to its tier, but also to be able to self-critique that very representation. It can become an ironic form of interplay where it is structured adversarial to what it connotes. We will notice two things happening in this environment: one is that it retains the foremost representational structure according to its tier, as well as a dissimilar function which distinguishes itself from that very representation to give the effect of self-reflection.

For instance, religion in the first tier would act as a regular locality that represents itself in a first tier, but then within that very domain, there is a distinctiveness that helps one reflect upon that very experience of representation. The problem with these liminal domains is that they are actualized as simply a first-tier representation, but they do contain a conceptual necessity of self-reflection that gives it a certain indispensable attribute. However, the important note is that it is a conceptual experience; it is not an embodied representation of self-reflection, but rather it is an embodiment of a representation according to its tier, as well as a conceptual overlay that allows one to self-reflect and find the nuances within that very experience.

A structural environment that does not elicit the same conceptual overlay as its representational theme, such as being in a single tier while providing a conceptual overlay of another tier, for example, a religion, creates a conflict. Within the presiding parameters of a first tier, by default of its conceptual overlay being a traditionalist framework, one cannot perform a structural environment within that surrounding setting, for it would be against that tier of representation. Thus, we have the result of a conflict between the embodiment experience and the conceptual overlay.

While it might be offering a nuanced approach and the material is surely an advantage point of perspective and we cannot deny that it is a form of self-reflection that gives credence to elements that a first-tier representation cannot do, it is still merely a conceptual experience. This would mean that one is not fulfilling the embodiment of that representation so that as the mind acknowledges the information, the permeation throughout the psyche does not take effect. This is why religious frameworks within the first tier will be almost ill-considered for the religious ideologies and rather seem like a plethora of surface information. The individual is completely a participant in the broader environment and only in a certain secretive notion of theory do they encompass the material of that framework.

The only matter in which they can become, whether it is by identity, embodiment, or permeation of psyche, to be the material of that conceptual overlay is through participating in second-tier environments that have the possibility of offering a representational reflection upon the representation in the first tier. The problem being, a religious framework, for instance, already espouses a certain conceptual system, so it cannot merely apply the availability of representation upon representation without any regulation. Instead, the religious framework in the second tier performs the same service of being a representational structure of the second tier while enabling a third-tier environment for the possibility of self-reflection of the second tier. No longer do they have the ability to reflect upon the first-tier environment; rather, their representational structure as a second tier performs as a third tier to self-reflect, still lacking the embodiment of that conceptual overlay and instead performing dutifully as a second-tier representation. Being that it espouses a conceptual overlay that only seeks to reflect the second-tier environment, it does not do well as a performative structure for second-tier happenstance and only becomes worthwhile as a learning environment.

As in any system in which there is disparity between the conceptual overlay and its tier of representation, the performative benefit will be primarily as an educational experience, much like the activation of a school environment. For an educational institution, it performs according to its tier because it cannot decompress from that environment, yet still activates a conceptual overlay as a third tier to reflect on that environment. Of course, there is the material, the educational material, which is a conceptual framework that does not necessarily have anything to do with the second-tier environment. But because the only ability of relevance in the social realm is to be part of the lineage of representation, if it walks away from the second tier, it automatically becomes a third-tier reflection of that representation.

However, it is not embodied; therefore, the educational institution is not an embodied experience, at least in the sense of being third-tier with the educational framework, and instead, becomes a learning experience that is not participating in social relevance. The memory, at least the existential memory of the experience in educational institutions, is merely the performance of that environment according to its tier, whether first, second, or third. The reason it has the ability to imprint memory at a higher depth than other locales is because the usage of the conceptual overlay has the realm itself act as a reflection of itself.

By being self-reflective, it places the experience of its afforded care into a perpetuating cycle of embodiment, particularly only to the embodiment of its tier and with nothing to do with the conceptual overlay. The conceptual overlay only provides the landscape to self-reflect on the surrounding tier, and indeed, by being a self-reflection environment, it perpetuates itself to experience itself.

Much like a religion in the first tier, it becomes a stronger sense of embodiment in that environment as a first-tier locale because the conceptual overlay compels it to self-reflect, and once there is self-reflection, a critique of the entire system forces the perspective to collect itself. However, the embodied experience that is noticed is not true in the sense of being first-tier, for it was only created through reflection of itself and thus becomes a false positive of embodiment.

The truth of the matter is that the embodiment is a real experience, only that it has gained it through putting the experience itself on a platform to reflect upon itself, thus offering completeness to the perpetual cycle of embodiment of that tier, something not available in regular environments. However, if we study self-reflection at a further depth, we notice that it is not a performative representation to the lineage of the representational format; instead, it is a disruption of the entire social process and speaks to the shadow of that representation. By self-reflecting, as with any self-reflection, one takes the entire entity of inquiry and dismembers it as if it were an incompetent and problematic system. The entire inquiry, to gain its initial sequence from the social system, is the performance of its vulnerabilities; in truth, all self-reflection is the activation of the shadow of the entity of inquiry.

This point is important in the field of psychology, which is inherently a self-reflection platform and indulges vulnerability as its premise, activating the shadow of individuals and society as if it were the reality of the entity and the social process. This is why biblical studies have never been merged with religious figures: the former approaches from a self-reflective place, activating the vulnerabilities of the system, which naturally dissipates the religious experience as a real and complete entity.

Therefore, it is notable that anyone who proceeds to understand contextual information at a fundamental level may be called a critic. They are not critical in the sense of being disruptive, but the entire performance of this memory and entity is the activation of its shadow in order to understand its fundamental basis and enter back into its performative light. Therefore, the educational institution is merely the embodiment of the shadow of its own representation and is not participating in the experience of true social animation.

Chapter Three: Representations and Psychology

Section One: The Interplay of Representation and Interaction in the Psyche

There is going to be a psychological reality that supersedes something structurally confined, inasmuch as we recognize that the psyche is only what it is by its alignment with reality. We are often reminded of the feral man, who, in a single generation, loses the capability of speech, never to attain it again. If speech is lost, we can presume that the faculties of the psyche are fairly limited and more associated with a mammal than with a human. When we discuss an interactive locale, there is a requirement from the external and perceptual realm to provide that experience, which can then be a regenerative process despite the structural environment. One can experience an interactive moment that is solely the validation of the current psyche contents, even when inhabiting a center locale. However, there is still the matter of bodily function required to allow that to happen. If the senses are participating in what surrounds them, they will overwhelm interactivity, resulting in representational interactivity which, if coerced to remain as such, would cause one to turn into the shadow of that environment.

The reason the center locale emanates information based on a representational format is the complex unification between structural reality and its container for information. As we approach the center locale, all information becomes representational, and all sociality is engineered to effectuate that process. There is still the possibility of being a representation outside the center locale, but it either would be the recreation of consciousness, where recognition just outside that realm is subpar relative to the center locale, which is more sophisticated than one's musings, or a group, for that matter. Yet, with all things, there is always an element of consciousness or representational activity that allows interactivity to continue.

When we dictate the notion of interactivity, we do not mean complete validation, because that is impossible. To validate something at its exact level would not enable a mirror-like function, and only when there is a curvature does a reflection occur. This deviation is the representation aspect, which allows for that validation. The degree of that curvature is the amount of representational activity versus validation. At the far end of the spectrum is representational activity, akin to that of the center locale, which does require a small amount of validation to be relatable but is otherwise beyond it. At the nearest end of the spectrum is validation, which is so alike that it provides little in terms of validation because of its similarity. When something is most similar, like two chairs of exactly the same formation, they do not validate each other because there is no pedestal from which one informs the other. Therefore, there is a requirement to retain a certain representational aspect to provide validation. Localities will mirror that spectrum according to their access to the center locality. When a locality deviates in either direction, either being more representational than its surroundings or more validating than its natural representation, it loses structural cohesion.

Consider a house: there is the restroom, which is least representational of the layout. If one sought to provide a stronger sensibility of representation to the restroom, it would lose its ability to perform alongside the rest of the structure. Two outcomes may occur: either the rest of the structure will take upon itself aspects of the restroom, especially its natural inclination toward interactivity, or there will be a lack of comfort in performing the biological tasks of the restroom because the representational activity does not align with that. Similar to how one may lose sleep when ruminating with a stream of consciousness, which does not provide rest and interactivity; biological functions lose their coherent space in the system.

Now consider the other side: the dining area, which is the most representational of the rooms. If it were not to take upon a stronger sensibility of representation, it would become interactive like the rest of the structure. The entire structure would now be without a representational head and, being fairly limited, would be more engineered for interactivity than for representation. This may be intentional, that one chooses to use the structure for interactivity instead of representation, for the benefits it serves. Additionally, we must consider what is outside this house and the localities it is embedded within, as the amount of representational activity must align with its surroundings. If it exceeds its embedded state, the surrounding environment will take upon itself that demand for representation, which is not the amount given to it. The ultimate outcome is a seclusion of consciousness created anew against the reality of civilization. The other option is that the course will be corrected: in the push for more representational activity than its embedded format, the external reality will demand its formation, and thus the house will be exemplified and mirrored to match the surrounding environment and, ultimately, civilization. Like the restroom, the house will be imposed upon by its environment to ignore its interactive elements and take upon the locality that surrounds it. It will not be able to inform more than that locality because it has overreached its representational activity and now spends all its time realigned with the current system, against what is beyond it.

Nevertheless, the psyche can maintain an interactive position even when surrounded by representational activity but must contain the perceptual and sensual domain. Similarly, one can theoretically endure a representational activation even when the surrounding environment is interactive, but must create cohesion between those two realities. Until then, there would be a conflict that prevents connection, as one represents the leadership of representational information and the other represents interactive aspects seeking validation based on a dosage of representational activity not aligned with it.

Section Two: Actualization and the Cyclical Process of Representation and Interactivity

Although there is a concept of structural environments and the actualization of each in accordance with their level of conscious depth, it is the case that there is a psychological process that precedes them. Hopefully, our inquiry will lead to the convergence between the psychological happenstance and the structural reality, and this will be the conclusion of this study. As we have noted, there are two primary components to deciphering a structural environment and two secondary components. The two primary ones are in service to opposite extremes. The first is the central locale, which is for the purpose of actualization and leads the conscious substance that becomes necessary for all other components. The second is the interactive realm, as this is the locale that allows for the validation and interaction of specific parts of its system without involving the wholesome nature of the system. In other terms, the wholesome endeavor versus the differentiation.

Now, for the psychological happenstance, we are already aware that there is the generality of perspective, the wholesome encounter, and the differentiation, which allows for the critical focus of a specific part of a system. However, this is not enough of an interpretation, because we have dictated that any actualization in the department of the central locale will be the direction of all differentiation, so that any wholesome interpretation of the psyche does not take the effect of dissemination to all the differentiating possibilities. Instead, it is more of a symbiotic relationship, where there is a turn to generality and onward to differentiation, each in service to the other. Actualization is the term that is more significant here, in which the psychological system can actualize and halt its actualization.

Generality is closely associated with actualization, but they are not from the same source. One can be general, such as the idea of all humans, but still not actualize themselves as participating in the idea in an existential manner to which they become that idea. Instead, we will always find generality that comes alongside actualization, but not the opposite. Actualization occurs when the psyche takes the existential state and places it upon the informational happenstance. This occurs naturally in the higher conscious realm, as would in the center locale, because one mirrors the environment so that they notice the degree of existential depth and accept that the information outside is more developed than the internal system. A psychological system is based on a certain actualization which, at one point or another, was recognized as more so than the current model.

Similar to a structural environment in which actualization is the most directive and competent aspect of the environment, the individual will naturally process and flow in the direction of higher levels of consciousness. With every encounter of the environment or individual, one will become a part of that consciousness. Consciousness becomes a natural process in which one synchronizes with the environment or with sociality, and there is a very complex process to halt this natural direction. However, there is the matter of the psychological system, in which it does follow a set of parameters so that consciousness is still a chosen event. One can technically actualize whatever they see fit, only by choice, choosing to existentially attach not to what is conscious substance, but more so a possibility of a specific direction. If we are to accept that one can actualize any idea, individual, or environment, then it demonstrates that the process of actualization can be chosen, whether when the environment demands it or when it does not.

To actualize something is to determine the current setting of processes in which one takes the leadership to reflect those processes upon the area of actualization so that it can incur the resemblance and thus direction of change. Actualization cannot occur where the regular system simply takes on new information. If such is in direction of regular dynamic exchange, then it is not an actualization but an addition of interactivity. As well, actualization cannot occur where one dismisses the current interactivity in order to participate in a new display of experience and information, for the current system does not have the bandwidth to properly engage in that realm.

Therefore, actualization occurs when we take the current system and have it reflect and represent itself in the new realm so that it can lead to a certain upgrade, which both interacts with the current system as well as reaches beyond it to an entirely new realm. The information is being used to reflect and represent simply as a bridge, which does not require following the rules of dynamic exchange nor veering off to a new realm with no participation in the current one. Even if one were to dismiss the current interactivity, the actualization will reach to the database of interactivity because it requires a semblance of recognition in order to understand and participate in the new realm.

Representation is the bridge of actualization, which becomes an anomaly when one chooses to actualize an event that is already in participation with their interactivity, as it should represent itself with its own information. One will need to glorify in order to act as if it were a new environment so that the actualization could take effect, in that the representational activity follows the current information. This becomes the glorification of selfhood, where the current interactivity becomes represented to invigorate itself, only by virtue of it being proposed for more than it is. This makes it a cyclical process because this coerced actualization dismisses current interactivity as insufficient, to re-participate in a new system which is only the same conscious substance, so that one chases their own tail. They dismiss the competency of their internal state in order to actualize that very same competency, so that they are able to maintain themselves through actualization that both dismisses the internal state and reinvigorates that very system. This is what occurs when one actualizes any interactive domain after the fact of its initial actualization. They maintain a status quo by this perpetual cycle, which seems to do little damage other than wasting time, but can be detrimental to an individual who has already participated in a more sophisticated realm, for these actualizations are a disruption to higher competency.

We will propose a direct example to make this explicitly clear. A very distinct form of interactive material would be one's childhood sentiment toward their parents. This is interactive to the adult, but at one point was actualized to be interactive, with preliminary interactive material behind it. As we do not need to be microscopic about the depths at which it reaches, we will accept the current sentiment to be the adult that is containing interactive substance of details between themselves and their parents. Note that this material is not re-realized or altered in any manner, and the sentiment in childhood is retained in the exact format in adulthood, with the only exception being that there is a perimeter around that interactive material because of one's development. At this point in adulthood, such interactivity remains at the bedrock of the system and remains fixated like the sun, with the planets interacting with it. The reason it does not change, while other surrounding interactivity can interact with it and change, is that alternative interactivity is seeking validation, for which it will change for realignment.

In this example, when the adult meets another person, they will relate to that person in accordance with those childhood relationships. They will be coerced into the definite forms that preceded them, so that the current interactivity is only a validation to its most relatable aspect in that past. The reason that this interactivity has the ability to change while the one preceding it does not is because the recent interactivity is utilizing a certain aspect of reflection and representation from the onset. Instead of viewing the current interactivity as pure, it is a mix of both representing the parental sentiment and also purporting its similarity as an interactive validation. When we remove the representational effect from the current relationship, it becomes more fixated, and thus a semblance of the parental experience in a more genuine format. There is no longer an attempt at alignment, but rather it is acted upon as if there is a relationship between that sentiment and the current one, so that they validate each other. In this way, there is an influential change between the old sentiment and the current one based on that dynamic. However, because the perfected validation would have one reimagine the entire landscape of the childhood experience, although the change would be forthcoming, a disruption of adulthood would incur. In effect, the child will be re-actualized.

This is why it is only natural for the adult to mix-use representational aspects and interactivity, so that the representation has the new relationship take the effect of an actualization in the current development, and the interactivity has the ability to slightly alter and develop the interactive convergence. This is why it takes the arduous and lengthy task to commence a new family body, for it is a constant negotiation between representational activity and thus a recreation and validation of interactivity, which moves along that sentiment. There is no method to shorten the process, for the direct interactivity would cause one to alter and proceed in the childhood activity, but without any ability to retain the present development, and all success would be a decline in the outcome. The same can be said for an overuse of representational activity, which would have no procedure of interactivity and be viewed as objects of environment for one's actualization without any semblance of interactive growth. While this is not inherently detrimental, if one does not have a procedure for their interactive semblance, then the later actualizations will be based on infantile sentiments and their reflections, so that the sophistication will be a dramatic impulse of a child in complex clothes, where it lacks surrounding education and sociality, for the detriment of society in the final accounting. One detracts from individuality, the other from society and sociality.

The memory of consciousness in relation to direct consciousness seems similar but are of a different class of capability with distinct parameters. One can theoretically perpetuate any memory upon any structural existence to bring about a resurgence of that consciousness. Even a desert, especially in a primary instance, will be viewed as it would within a consciousness perspective since the familiarity of the landscape of the individual is secured to that prior system and its memory. Of course, this is fabricated, for how could there be consciousness within a desert, all without structure or sociality? Yet the first time one views it, there is nothing to compare besides a memory of consciousness to layer upon it, as if there were a showing in the museum of a desert landscape.

We constantly perform this act, using memory to apply to a new system, whether it holds greater or lesser substantiation of consciousness, as in the case of the desert. When one applies a memory to an inferior structural setting, they may perceive this locale as emanating more consciousness than that of its true nature. If in present it is actualized for the individual, they become the recipient of the desert as if it were of substantial consciousness, which then replaces the source of the memory and its sincere consciousness. The individual becomes the embodiment of the desert, even though it does not contain any consciousness. The vitality is only in how a consciousness system would manifest such within its domain, much like an art installation of a desert in a museum.

They may act out the characteristics of the desert against the memory of real consciousness, where one becomes their own enemy, perpetually downgrading the psyche. We can even view this as psychological degeneration, which, over a prolonged period, cannot be reversed.

Structural consciousness is a representational structure and consequently can be found in any environment. This allows us to have the desert represent itself in complete form despite its lack of structure.

However, this does not mean it is true in its nature, for it represents a prior memory that allows for that representation. If one is raised within a desert, they cannot have a representational element in affordance to it because it does not correlate to something of more vitality than the sand of that space.

Presumably, representation represents itself to a substantial marker; therefore, it is not the thing itself because it is a representation; a pattern that leads back to a source. However, even the source itself is a representation but aligned with the thing itself in a structural element. In other words, without the source material prior to reaching the desert locale it would constitute a true desert. Rather now that there is prior source material, which consists of complex systems, the desert becomes a representational element. It is those things, in their representation, that are now being highlighted. These elemental things are also representations but are connected to a structural system that emanates toward that very propensity. In our case, we can find that the desert is usually representational of the source material about the expansiveness possible within consciousness. It is the source material itself, however, consciousness and its structural element, that teaches its origin, nature, and necessity, giving rise to the feeling of the need for expansiveness.

Usually, when one is most attached to a source and its central form of consciousness, they are most aware of the necessity or recognition of the need for expansiveness due to the rigid and strict nature of consciousness. It is most representational when one is most attached to a prior state of consciousness.

Any locale can serve as a form of representation, for if a desert can, so can anything that contains any meager structure or sociality. The difference between source material and representation lies in how the representational element takes effect. If we enter a structural environment and it represents itself not for the sake of its reference to another locale or its source material, but because it stands on its own, then we can be sure that it is representing itself for the thing itself.

However, in most cases, the representational elements are simply leading back to a narrative of source material, which has now been elaborated in a certain format with nuances not seen within the structure itself. Since the source material cannot cover everything, nor provide a vantage point of its perspective because it is within itself, it remains possible for any locale to provide those elements.

One of the strongest representations for any locale is public stations, for they are representational of the viewpoint of the source material. They offer a perspective that could only be possible outside of the system, as it is possible to have an infinite number of perspectives upon the source material, as long as the station provides that representation.

Let us take the example further. Within the station, one can either view the representational element for itself, even as it retracts to source material, whether one has experienced it or not. This is because such is envisioned as existent with source material because the helm of consciousness is the development of life itself.

A child still views a station as reaching back to a form of consciousness allotted by available experience but is given sentiment toward figures or possibilities in the enlargement of affairs. This creates a stopgap or placement marker, but there remains a sentimental value toward the helm of consciousness until one experiences the inference toward its realistic structural environment. However, when that does occur, when one gains access to the source material, those prior place markers no longer hold credence. Even parental figures lose their sentimental value as helms of consciousness because no one has replaced them with their true structural value.

That does not mean that one has lost all sentimental recognition of parental figures as helms of consciousness because for the primary years of life they hold such a position. This layer requires constant fulfillment as one enlarges and expands, but it is only for the necessity of fulfilling those stages of life, not for the fulfillment of current progress in life.

One can place upon any structural environment the memory of a source material itself. Instead of allowing the present representational element to give credit to the source material, one can already provide that layer of memory as the source material, now allowing the availability of representational aspects in their influential form. The problem is that when one brings about the memory of the source material, they retain the traces of that conscious element, preventing them from allowing the representational elements in front of them to provide an inference. This is similar to how, if one has their parental figure side by side with their sibling, it is more difficult for the sibling to provide a representational element toward the parental figure because both are in the same system. One only sees their uncle or aunt through the lens of how they view their parental figure, instead of viewing them as an alternative perspective.

To take this example further, if the sibling is separated from the parental figure, they now become a representational element, but can be confused as the thing itself, rather than a simple informant upon the source material (the parental figure). Therefore, we require both systems to work together so that when they are separated, it is recognized that one comes from an aspect of connection to their parental figure which is now in sight of inquiry. This allows for a vantage point that is not the thing itself.

When the parental figure and sibling are together, one can conceptually separate them. Instead of viewing the parental figure in their perspective on the sibling, which is useful at intervals, one can view the sibling more loftily, as a vantage point to arrive at the thing itself. Thus, we replace the memory just enough to allow for a recognition of the source material, so that the representational elements do not simply reflect upon themselves as if they are a system of their own, but at the same time, allow for a separation between the source material and the representational elements on the ground, such that there is the ability for perspective without overburdening the system itself.

Intro-representational refers to a case when one interacts with a representational body as a point of direction that precludes and circumvents their representational position within that conjecture. Extro-representational is the opposite, namely, when one utilizes an existing representational body in the experience of exemplifying oneself as a modality in that arena, reflecting one's peculiar state.

The primary example of extro-representational form is the appearance of political representation, wherein one is assumed within the experience of that modality to embody the representational structure. Although it falls upon the individual to ascertain whether to engage with either criteria, whether to be extro and endure that modality, or intro, where the conjecture of political office or stature becomes arbitrary in accessing the whole representational spectrum.

It is only natural for one to lean toward extro, as it grants the stature of modality, encapsulating that representation and becoming part of that spectrum. Although the opposite does occur having encapsulation become a beholding of experience of that modality, which does not allow for interaction with it, nor for engaging with the broader spectrum of representations. In essence, it becomes devoid of all representation due to its intrinsic isolation.

The experience is the only element that remains animated in this process, but only for as long as that modality is constituted by external sociality, which serves to bridge the loss of one's innate ability to connect with its possibility. When external sociality determines the degeneration of that representational element, then one may even lose that experience, or the modality itself, thus facing full exposure to an abyss of representational elements.

Even when experience itself is preserved through an animating sociality, it would still lack a particular nuance. Beyond consisting without discourse, restricted to observational vantage, it would also signal the loss of individuality. For in taking the stage of this encapsulation, and being without intrinsic self-awareness, individuality becomes only a canvas for maintaining that representational element.

Intro representation has the effect of providing a personalized direction towards the spectrum of representation without granting individual modality within it. This seems an impossibility, for without a modality of being as a representational element, -without the experience of being a citizen of the state, --without the experience of being a participant of that embodiment, one would not be able to interact with the entirety of that spectrum. Foremost one has to become beholden to a form of personality that is given the right towards interaction, and without such, one would be lost to a general criterion for the basis of interaction.

Meaning to say, before any interaction can occur, it requires an embodiment of the general structure, so that there is something intrinsic to personhood that allows for a continuity of interaction. One would need to embody representational elements before they intend to interact such, and attempting to interact without that embodiment would be futile and generally untethered to individuality; and thus mostly a proclamation of interaction rather than an experience of such.

We are going to enter by way of an example, and this will be more structurally apparent but is just as well applicable to social circumstances. In a case where people are in a cave, to which they all came from land and now residing inside and have no access to land. Within that small organization, there are going to be three partitions of that group: one will be the general masses, one will be the representatives of those masses, and a third would be those containing intro-representational of the memory of land and its future possibility.

Those who represent the general modality of the group experience as well as the dynamic of circumstance will be extro-representational figures. For it is they that produce for that society the experience of its structure and circumstance. For them, they do not gain access to any further representational elements beyond the cave, and they are without individuality, so that they serve as an abridgement of the circumstance to which they find themselves within.

They are lost from the processing of their exemplification; meaning they do not intrinsically understand how they have enacted purposeful representation, although they do understand the parameters of such. The parameters will include but be limited to their individuality, which becomes represented, the sociality of that group, and the intersections of these two. One will always represent themselves through the particulars of their individuality, which are assisted by a representational theme within society. Society, in turn, will follow the individuality to which a representational theme has been attributed, as society is composed of individuals who relate to each other through their unique individuality.

They have also given full detachment from possibility and the representational elements in regard to land, because they are willingly participants of the encapsulation of concurrent circumstances. Therefore, they are more detached from land than anybody within the cave, and that is the sacrificial element to their being. Every experience of representing as that modality keeps them further from connection to representations upon land, so that in some sense they also fail to represent what is contained within the structure.

The general sociality of the cave does maintain a connection to representational elements on land, which the extro-representational beings are now expected to encapsulate. It is not necessarily the case that this general sociality will align with their personal experience of extro-representational themes, but rather that such alignment is merely assumed. It is not that they reject how one represents themselves within a society, but that the mere existence of the extro-representational element would naturally cause the experience to occur. In some cases, the representational element serves a purposeful role in the objective of sociality, while in other cases, it is presupposed or arbitrary. For now, it is only the modality of experience that the extro beings are seeking, rather than the purposeful objective of any extro-representational form, whether that be to transition into intro, or to provide a representational conjecture that is beneficial to that sociality.

The former, that of representing themselves in that circumstance, so that they may interact with that sociality through the experience of embodying that duress is the natural process within the dynamic between extro and intro. It is how a child first begins with an embodiment of as a representational element of their parents but then begins to move away from that and become intro and thus interact with the familial structure as would an individual. At the point of being extro instead of intro, one makes themselves an idolization of the system or environment to which they present themselves to. The young child presents themselves as a structured being and distinction to the familial body. They become representational for external inquiry, but in purpose of themselves, they are not experiencing such a representation but rather take up the stance of being like an advertisement that does not have a self-regulating system but holds itself in inference to something else.

The child commences in this path because they are offering themselves to the familial body as an organic banner to make aware of their presence and significance for the homebody. They do not have the mechanisms to interact in an external fashion, and until that process is enabled, they function by being a stabilization of familial inquiry. Their process of growth arises when the familial body and its dynamical constituents feel compelled to interact with that bannered force of significance and through that exchange, the child begins to receive the necessary information that allows them to understand in a manner that builds the mechanisms for further interaction.

In the example of the advertisement, it is the lack of selfhood in the advert, but yet the inference that is allowed towards the onlooker that has one interact with the advertisement because of that inference and its material, to a point where the advertisement gains in awareness of selfhood by that consonant interaction. With that selfhood, it would be on the basis of the inference material such that now the advertisement understands itself based on its dynamical exchange of that material, which then can jumpstart with the possibility of interaction outside that sphere of inference.

The objective of extro-representational stature is for the complete idolization that has all dynamical inferences play the part of interacting according to that representational model. It is in this hope that through the diversion of selfhood or complete expense of interaction, the external dynamics will give back in a manner that will teach them the basis of that exchange. Once that exchange is received, no longer do they need to be a representational model and contrast to the environment, but rather the environment has begun to teach them their intrinsic substance. At present they could interact with the substance as if they were a third-party viewer upon themselves. In this case, they begin to have the perspective of the onlooker to a point where they now can become interactive and available to the foresight of elements that do not pertain to the specific conjecture of their purposeful representational model. At its furthest point, they begin to lose the modality of being an idolization of the environment and now have the benefit of generally interacting with the entire environment from an individualized vantage point that does not have a modality in itself. (Generally speaking, since there is always a certain modality)

Within a competent dynamical group, it does require an individual or portion to represent themselves in contrast to the system. Naturally, there will be those that do not agree with the fulfillment of direct interaction, thereby succeeding the only option of presenting themselves in contrast to that environment, thus placing themselves on a pedestal to be the banner of that experience, however, in a contrasting manner. Sometimes, it is not only those least agreeable to the system who do so, but also individuals who, instead of interacting, willingly choose to become the embodiment of that environment. The child who begins their journey as a representation of the systemic structure, rather than interacting with it, is not doing so out of disagreement with the system, but rather because they seek to fortify their position, trusting that there will be enough dynamical inferences to allow them to construct a sense of selfhood to the point where they can begin to interact properly.

Without the presupposition of becoming the extro-representational model, one will not have enough dynamical exchanges that will construct a criteria to begin intro-representational development. At times, some individuals will not follow the course towards an intro-representational process but instead choose to be the expense of their individuality for the performance of the system. Alternatively, as we mentioned, in the case of disagreement towards the system of their partaking endeavor, they will automatically become the modality that contrasts themselves against that environment. Or in another case, it is the dread of existential development or participation, which has one set themselves apart from the environment and become extro-representational.

However, the only purposeful objective in terms of internal development is for the intersection between extro and intro, as is the case of a child. We would never want the mature version of the child to then lead back into extro-representational models within the familial body, for they have already obtained enough exchange that it is within their scope to continue interacting from an individualistic standpoint. Of course, in the case where the mature child does not agree with the familial body or circumstance will begin to become the extro-representational model, or if they are unwilling to participate in the existential development, they will remain extro-representational. They do not gain knowledge or development under the arrest of being the idolization of a system, but they do have the benefit of being on the receiving end of that exchange, although mostly of the negative proportion. Because they exist as the contrast and use the environment to represent themselves above or beyond it, they will embody the system's idolization material, which will be somewhat negative in nature.

Although we do find that individuals can embody the extro-representational model and claim to embody the positive attributes of the environment, by default, being beholden to the contrast of the environment means that it is actually negative, though only perceived as positive. There is no ability for one to be extro-representational and receive the positive effects of an environment, for the entire process is to set themselves apart to behold and contrast, for they are not internal to the system but rather utilize the material to offer substance of their orientation to interact in dynamical proportion, which can only occur in contrast and not by interaction.

Corresponding to the individual who is extro-representational in the cave, they cannot present themselves as oriented within the internal system because their entire mechanism is to demonstrate how they contrast that system, allowing them to perceive how they can encapsulate the environment while remaining set apart. This can only occur through the direct appropriation of what they contrast; thus, the negative aspect of the environment.

However, if the environment itself has a negative orientation or if there is prevailing dread in the cave, the individual with the extro-representational model will become the contrast to such and thus embody positivity to inspire courage. This is a common motif in challenging experiences, where individuals gain representational status by being the most courageous in promoting a positive notion against negative developments. Therefore, rather than viewing it as strictly positive or negative, it is merely contrast; although most of the time it will lean toward negative. If, however, we find it to be positive in orientation, we can assume the general consensus troubling which necessitates a representational model of positivity.

The intro-representational model is possible by virtue of the embedded forum that is supposed to surround the supposition to which it attempts to represent itself. Usually, the case would be that an identity platform is enabled to thus have the ability to represent itself within and be contained by the spectrum of that identity. For instance, a child would constitute an intro-representational theme toward the homebody identity, such that they are required to embed within the higher structure of the body in order to facilitate their unique representational platform.

From the perspective of the child, it is possible that they remove themselves from the embeddedness of the homebody identity, which is a natural process of mature development, in which they will become separate from the possibility of representing themselves as a child, for they are not within the homebody to become a child of the homebody.

However, the parental figures do not have that same element of representing themselves within the homebody because they are the progenitors of the homebody to the point where they become external processes that enable and disable the possibility of its internal process. They are not part of the identity in its fundamental sense; therefore, they cannot represent themselves within and contained by the homebody, but rather require a broader embedded structure in which they can represent themselves and their attachment to the homebody, such as when they bring the homebody outside of the familiar structure, which now has the opportunity to represent itself according to the identity that is afforded to the parental figures.

It is not always the case that the parental figures represent the homebody in a broader identity structure, but only when they are embedded into an identity structure and facilitate their representational model within that space. If either of these two requisites are not met, either they do not have an identity that is beyond the spectrum of the body, or they choose not to represent themselves within that structure, whether by choice or by the very fact that the parental identity is not interested in that aspect, they will, in fact, not participate with the body as a representational structure, either within itself or in broader realms.

Intro-representational models have a peculiar characteristic: they must avoid any reference outside the embedded identity structure, so that it automatically anticipates their representational theme within that hierarchy. More so, one is required to maintain a representational theme that fits with the embedded identity, so that a child is required to fit the role that is requisite for the child according to the identity of that homebody. The child also avoids the premonition of viewing anything external to the homebody, so as not to dissipate the embedded identity structure and thereby lose their representational model. Thus, we find robust adherence of a child to the familiar structure in order to keep and maintain the identity of the homebody and continue to represent themselves within the structure.

The reason for the strong adherence to the representational model is that one gains and sustains their vitality through the modality of the representational structure. It is from this that they access the experience of consciousness for themselves. The child gains a preliminary stage of consciousness through the representational aspect that is afforded to them within the familiar structure. It is possible that the child will access consciousness from other arenas, but in accordance with their disposition to follow the representational model, they will continue to abide by that structure so as to continue with the experience of consciousness that the identity structure, in this case, the familial body, provides as a habitat of vitality.

Access to genuine consciousness is possible because the embedded identity structure is a habitat within the broader scheme of public exposure, such that the homebody is an identity within that sphere. Therefore, the child, also embedded within the homebody and having no recollection of what is beyond it, will still gain access to consciousness because of the presumed and accurate assumption that the identity of the homebody represents itself in a broader spectrum of affairs.

Chapter Four: Imitation and Modeling

Plato asks a question: will there come a day when poetry will be explained with more thorough arguments, and then we will abandon our premise regarding poetry? Poetry is the art expression of language and must be regarded for the art form itself as well as the language additives that are irrespective of the art form. If we were to say that poetry is an imitation of the existential state, to which there is a conceptual overview to reference and supersede those experiences, then we also must conjure an application for poetry in the development of language and more so to the internal dialogue which contrasts the happenings of the psyche.

Although one may endure a psyche experience, without the language to decipher one aspect from another it will become a wholeness of movement without any control of the specificity of that arrangement. In this context, language is the mode of operation to detail the occurrences of the psyche so that we can compartmentalize the various complexities with precision to enable the oversight of its movements.

Language provides an internal decoder of the psyche and thus is not a process of the psyche, but the psyche as understood to its truer reality. When we engage in a poetic verse, we allow for language to follow existential variation or biological reality, which in turn allows the psyche to enable its parts through having a literal world for it. Until we gained language for psychoanalytic developments, those experiences were experienced without the degree of nuance that would be appropriate for such subtlety. Anxiety is only experienced as anxiety because of the various developments of language which allow for the psyche to understand the components which make up anxiety. We may think it to be a very developed view of the psyche, but rather it is the language which has adapted to those components which allow for the experience. Although we need grand theories to advance language so that it more accurately reflects reality, if anxiety were not an inherent part of that reality framework, the continual refinement of definitions would not amplify it as an existential experience of the psyche.

The ironic notion of anxiety is that as we seek to handle and ultimately drive those components of the psyche, it only grants us a more elaborate language which in turn opens to new subtleties of the anxiety component of the psyche. In a sense, anxiety outpaces itself, to reveal more than it can handle until we culminate or exhaust its definition for a proper resting period to occur. Reality is as it is, and surely the end of a certain component of the psyche will be assured when it reveals its aspects across the continuum. However, the development of one component of the psyche will demand a rebalancing of the others, so that what will be exhausted for the moment will require to be revisited according to the other developments of the psyche.

For instance, masculinity and femininity are a great exploration of recent centuries, so much so that we can say that in certain forms they have been revealed to the point of exhaustion. However, because they are so near to the central existential nature of the psyche, they become points of return upon every reflection or development of the psyche. We could call them central themes which, as the psyche develops, will become more important points of return and never less.

We could view all psychoanalytic developments as a sustainable learning period because we are prescribed to revisit subtle aspects of the psyche, although infantile, which are presently demanding of the progress of society. It provided a niche for the psyche which had advanced to new territory, making it necessary to return to baseline existential moments, especially those of childhood for the rebalance of the psyche. Because everything is based on preliminary states, as the overall expansion occurs, each of those states becomes again relevant to produce a more nuanced perspective for the advantage of continued systems. If this does not occur, where advancements do not revisit such infantile states, the wholeness of the system will exhaust itself. Instead, those infantile unaddressed states will require more and more attention. They will be reluctantly dragged along for more expansion which has them take the role of the whole system. The end result is that one grows into the infantile state even as they seem to be advancing new frontiers, and they begin to act like a sophisticated child.

Yet, this does not prove effective if we do not have the keys to enter into these zones of the psyche, either because we do not have a theory or because we are lacking language. A lack of theory would be if we did not have the psychoanalytic theory to behest the adult from resuscitating these crevices of psyche material that are deeply layered and formatted.

Without language, we would not retain an internal dialogue of sophistication to follow the new aspects that are not known to the preliminary states themselves. The child never contained the vocabulary of such nuanced language of anxiety, yet the visitation of those states requires an adult standard that will be able to enter into proper dialogue at the later instance. We cannot internally converse with the language of a child, especially in concern of the areas which have been articulated. Instead, we need to decipher the code of the infantile material so that it can be used to advance the mature adult.

Without language, we only have states that can be revisited through psyche work but do not grant the ability to advance its foothold through material enlargement, which is the importance of the mature mind. The theory will bring the individual into those realms and may even contain a process of revealing its substance for enlargement but will fall short of social language which can reveal those colors that will make for an articulation of mature internal dialogue. Theory highlights the concept of anxiety, while language will define anxiety with the nuance needed for adequate articulation.

The anxiety that has been more defined was not by theory but through social development of the definition itself and will be an available thoroughfare to have one understand its underpinnings. The early psychoanalytic theories did not understand anxiety's true definition but rather had the access point of a logical continuum which led to psyche relations of anxiety. The relations cannot be unfolded by theory; they will evolve over time in the continuous use of theory. Until a much later date, when anxiety became defined and refined, it became the revealing of the psyche process itself, which would be the practical ramification of any theory of the psyche.

When we define language, we are using the psyche's understanding of its definition and not the termed definition. For the instance above, the concept or terminology of anxiety as it has developed has become a database of material for its simple definition. To truly follow the social definition of anxiety as it has evolved would require a proper thesis of its own. We only retain a simple definition to equalize all the language under a system, but it is the case that certain words contain a vast library of material for their definition.

This is where poetic language becomes the manifest material of providing that nuance. Poetry imitates the existential states that have been provided by theory. The psychoanalytic theory has provided a framework in which the art expressions of many forms have taken up the cause of bringing about the relations to those substitutions. Indeed, the form of poetry itself has allowed for the language to be defined and relatable to the psyche processes so that theory can be articulated and thus truly interacted with.

This is the case for all our art forms, which do provide that provision of granting the imitation or rather the language of those developments. Without the language or these art forms, what comes about is a threshold of psyche movements that cannot be conversed or related to. We could say that art form is an inevitable result of the advancement of theory and thus need not be discussed, for individuals will always repossess what has been told through existential experience. However, it is the degree of disparity that may be of concern.

A theory can last generations without having an existential articulation or definite language in the form of imagery or words that will make it a relatable substance. It would sit in the background in its repressed state, originally to the specific scientific endeavors, without being available to social or internal discourse. We may say that normal social discourse would develop itself to be coupled with advances of language according to the ruminating theories or progress of the psyche.

However, through the history of civilization, this proves to be untrue. The psyche may advance to far points but will not have tools in social discourse to invent imagery or language that provides adequate articulation of these new frontiers. Indeed, the advancements that are made through theory or through psyche enlargement or consciousness are done not through relatability but through logical suppositions. In terms of its own relatability, it does not have tools at its disposal to provide an existential experience of what has been unearthed. Moreover, social discourse will not be able to invent such suppositions because it is bound to the prior language in reference to the imitation that was portrayed for social consumption. The only matter of granting language and imagery to the suppositions is through art form or imitation. It must be imitated because, precisely being unavailable for true understanding, it must be looked at through the lens of an attempt of imagination.

The existential experience of the theory is naught, and so we must use a tool that provides an outlook of what would be an existential experience if the theories were put to practical use. They are not in real time, and the art form denotes this by demanding social consciousness through its language.

In the most wrought scenario, without imitation of any sort, the theories and the progress begin to fade into the abyss, without retaining a social landscape to continue with a practical location in the psyche. The most troubling aspect is that, without these imitative foundations, they may no longer be recoverable as history moves in a different direction. For instance, literary criticism has made a thorough field of progress in its suppositions, but for reasons that vary, it has not been imitated in proper art forms to which the tradition has surpassed its material for others, to which it will never be revitalized as it could have been. In the scholarly field it may continue to progress, but because it has not been imitated in its due time, any attempt would disrupt the progress after the point. We sense such when entering its domain as if it is a nostalgic moment in which we do not have a memory of its relatability. It is very difficult to prove that this is the case, but we can acknowledge that it was not imitated in social forums and thus became archaic even as scholarship continues to thrive.

This is why science, which can be directed to objective application, is most sought, being that it will be imitated or applied in social discourse in due time. We may think that the application of science for technological advances is not an imitation yet in such a context it is. The object that has had theory applied to it will be, for the social realm, a visualization or representation of the theory in real time. The item stands for the theory, and although it has not been imitated for psyche processes, it does vitalize the theory. Much like how an architectural form can be a representation of complex theories even as it does not provide psyche material. It is upon the social realm to receive architecture to a degree that will foster relatability to the theory.

The same is for the object of scientific invention, which retains the theory so long as the object is practical to social relevance but does not produce the imitation of that theory within psyche material. Yet we can assume that if the object is relevant for an extended period, it will be a social instance that has psyche imitation attached. However, the medium from the object and the psyche resonance is through various art forms. Because the object is very practical, it enters into the simplicity of normal living and does not have the advantage of being an art form in itself.

We would like to say that every scientific invention is an art form to imitate the theory for existential appropriation. However, because the very object enters into a market exchange, it becomes an itemized aspect of social exchange. This would have the object become a representation of the easiest social application instead of the theory to which it holds. The object will be a representation in how it operates, or what it does, instead of what it is; it takes the role of the activity aspect of the psyche which is represented in arms, hands, legs, and feet. Although it does grant an imitative item of hands or doing as a universal element, it does not provide its most important aspect of imitating the theory which produced it.

We do not perceive the engine as an imitation of the theory of the power of fire but rather as an object for powerful mobility. Think of the language associated: what is the 'engine' that drives these affairs, meaning what is the central power of these affairs. It is imitated as the perceived outer body that moves without the awareness of a device that makes it move. This is the imitation of an outer body at work without being keen on its central power.

However, we do not find the language of an 'engine' being used to imitate the nature of fire when utilized in a certain manner. Even as that is the truest representation of the engine, it remains in the shadow. This is due to the utilization of the engine participating in the marketplace with such advocacy that it does not allow for a representation that is removed from such utility.

We can further on our own accord and represent the engine for its theory, but will be required to remove the utility of it. We would be interacting with the engine for its own sake irrespective of what it does. This would deflate the whole entity since we would not have a concern for engines without their utilization and thus would not seek them as representations. They become aesthetically unpleasing to fulfill the grand theory of fire, as they seem too complex and over-varied to provide such subtlety. Even our attempt at having the engine represent its theory has us find disfavor in its system as being an unruly manner of imitation. It does not seek to imitate with the respect of the whole human edifice in which all art forms must be considerate, for it is meant to be an existential represention even as it provides such detachment from human affairs of complexity. The engine is made up of varying parts that do not have a purpose in the representation of the theory. We cannot account for each part in assisting in the representation, especially when other facets can do so with poetic prose.

When a simple picture of the mystic nature of fire in combustion state would provide that sentiment, the engine would lose personal relatablity by having so much for that same sentiment. It will not be able to provide a reflection point, being that the overindulgence demands a representation of all of its parts, which is most reflective in accordance with what it does; like the troubling poem which, instead of representing its subtle theme, becomes a representation of drastic psyche movements. The theme is still available, but it is more accessible and thus reflective in its more abstruse sentiment of uncontrolled thinking.

If one were to need an imitation of chaotic thinking, one must not look further than underdeveloped art expression.

The reflection point is the thing that matters for this disparity, for what mirrors at its initial glance is going to decide for its representation. The engine, being a very itemized system that is working in unision, will invoke an initial mirror of its utilization. The first glance might notice a single part and have it represent something in relation, which then moves from item to item until the psyche does not perceive items but a system of items. Immediately the representation of the system becomes for whence it goes, for all systems must be embedded in other systems. This makes the initial mirror of the engine become a representation for what it does. Even the explanation of how the system works will be in accordance with its parts, gaining a whole dictionary for them. This still represents the itemized aspects in reference to the system as a whole.

This is the reason the engine is concealed in the first place, having the shame of not representing itself but as a system to another system of mobility. Had the engine not been concealed, then it would become a representation that is less lofty than its utilization. It would be represented by its lack of availability to represent its theory by being a system of utilization even as the theory does not dictate that. It would become a representation of a failure of theory to be imitated in the social sphere, in which it represents doing without being; almost as if the engine is a body without a mind, to which the social sphere would not will to gain representations of doing without being, like a chicken without its head. This is why we conceal the engine: to conceal its representation of its failure, to not be deterred by this sentiment. Nature works in this manner for our own body, for if revealed without the concealment of skin, it would represent in a similar manner as an engine that does not have a wholeness to it.

Yet, it is still society's existential need to have an imitation which produces the effect of the theory that is established to build the engine. This becomes a necessity because the theory of the power of fire in confined spaces ruminates the social sphere as long as the object is of use. We could reach a point where the engine is obsolete and thus the theory which is bound up to it also becomes a non-consequential theory.

This would permit us to exist without the imitation of that theory as long as there are no objects of combustion in social or market exchange.

Section Two: Modeling and Representations

Modeling in the criteria of representing the human body in a superior form is a great medium for understanding representations. The process is such that the object of modeling, in this case the human body, is perceived as a mobile force of agency. The mobility in whatever form the modeling has stimulated would correlate to a sequential setting of parts that make up a whole body. Without the appearance of a version of mobility, modeling would only appropriate a portion and not appear in the wholeness of human form. Even in the stagnation of posture, there is still a provoked representation that necessitates to take effect, which correlates to a propagation of the system of the human body.

The second criterion is the advent of finding the juncture points that are most stimulating for the representation of its form. Nakedness would not be enough, for it may be attributed to the shallow form of infancy in contrast to a shown nakedness. For this reason, there must be an element within nakedness to perform that function, with complete nakedness to be presumed as naivety; not in the performed function of naivety, the pitiful appropriation of what lies dormant in the human form.

However, this performance does not grant consequential inference points but only adheres to maintaining the aspect of being a performance of wholeness. The second point is what distinguishes ultimate modeling from its counterparts. This is the aspect of cultural sophistication onto which it is acting as the emphasizing material of modeling. The human form is most at its element in the height of bodily physique and psyche development. The physique is only possible to model if, in fact, there is an element of representation inherent in the individual performing the modeling. There is little cultural aspect, that is, psyche or conceptualizations, which partake in the selection of the physique. For it is the form of the human at its best, which finds itself from a psyche which exemplifies sexual primacy, health, genes, and other factors. Still, those elements are required to be modeled, which would be a performance of sexual primacy, health, and genes. The mobility in its various forms will account for that in its performance so that it is transparent that human form is represented at its ultimate.

However, the second inquiry, that of cultural sophistication, is also part of the modeling. If mobility is the sequence, then the junctures of the sequence are the cultural aspect. These are the ultimate aspects of global development which are exemplified in the modeling process. Such that it is not enough to model nakedness in a performing manner, but that there is a cultural context that is connected adequately to the moving pendulum. It is no coincidence that human modeling is inextricably linked to corporations or institutions, for any other manner would seem arbitrary. Even if an individual chooses to perform the modeling function, they are doing so within a cultural context, which, if part of a limited horizon, would feel out of place and may be deemed contrary to the intended performance.

The wholeness that is gained from mobility is owed to the representation of mobility itself. Anything that is mobile is considered whole, and stagnation is attributed to its parts. Take, for instance, a vehicle: its performance of mobility grants its association of being a complete vehicle. While in its stagnation, especially when unavailable to mobility, it is seen in its parts. An individual walking or running is taken by the wholeness of their system; when resting, they are assumed in their parts. The walking individual, especially when they are a stranger to us, is part of the mobile unit of mobile persons in the context of possible origins or destinations. There is little inquiry into aspects of their psyche which are not relative of walking, for the performance takes the whole appearance and has the person appear whole. When we perceive a resting stranger, we begin to dissect components that have little to do with the state of rest; instead, we find aspects of far-reaching depth, whether of persona, identity, or psyche. The same is even more applicable when an individual is running, for the probability that we follow aspects of their psyche which do not pertain to running is fairly low. The same would be for the individual within a mobile vehicle: we notice them as a continuation of the vehicle movement and find it difficult to follow aspects of them that are not consistent with that wholesome context. Mobility is considered a performance, and a performance is exemplifying the form of that which performs it. Resting is at a loss of performance and exemplifies its various parts according to the sway of attention. There is the possibility of resting as a performance, yet in most cases where resting is a state of immobility we take notice of its parts.

This is why the seated localities will always be more interactive, and mobile localities will always be more performative. By virtue of sitting, an attribute of rest, we notice wide-ranging aspects of an individual, which makes for a great venue for interaction. While in a state of mobility, the interactions are stretched and mostly associated with the context of that mobility. Any conversing other than the context of mobility will place a strain on the dialogue and will exhaust the proponents.

We notice a distinction with bodily exercise, in which there is applicable interaction on par with a resting situation. When we consider that exercise is not a mobile function but utilizes mobility for a resting function, then we clear up that disparity. Such mobility is not in context of an origin and destination, and appears less performative and more interactive, depending on the motive of the exercising individual, which can take a performative function, especially in a social setting. However, the activity of exercise that is not part of a social aspect is a criterion of mobility that does not take a performative function.

The same can be said for the objective of enjoying mobility itself, in contrast to the mobility function of origin and destination. However, even with all said, there is still a structural origin and destination, whether for exercise or the enjoyment of mobility itself. For this reason, exercise will begin to take a performative function, which the Hellenic civilization devoted towards.

Thereby, the choice is usually made to enter the performative function and find social settings that would interact with that performance. This is why exercise gravitates towards social settings, which then gravitates to the central localities of culture, as is the case for any performative function. When one adheres to the privatization of exercise, what begins to occur is a perpetuity towards exemplifying the exercised results in a performative manner. In this way, it can be considered performative enough for the recurring mobility in the privacy of their non-performative localities.

This is why intellectual inquiry is fairly difficult to come by in non-resting settings. The process of intellectual material is an interaction with portions or subjects that delineate the wholeness of personhood. Therefore, the mobile setting is adversarial to intellectual stimulation, for it constantly demands the wholeness of personhood, or at least the generalization that makes intellectual inquiry bland. We may find that there are certain forms of resting that bridge into a form of mobility. For instance, sitting at a station, which is a state of physical rest, abling in a locality that functions as a mobility. As well, sitting in public locales that have the majority as mobile constituents, for instance, the porch of a locality that intersects with public walking.

While we do find the public park to serve the immobile function, it happens to intersect with the mobility of its constituents, which makes it inhospitable to the true state of rest. Indoors offer a locality that makes it difficult for mobility by its confined structure, thereby leaning towards a state of rest. This is why most intellectual happenstance occurs indoors, for it serves a locality of immobility. The industrial locality will not serve as a locality of immobility, for its constituents are mobile in an unconfined manner, making the locality a mixture of structural immobility and proponent mobility. Thus, the ultimate state of rest is both structural immobility and proponent immobility.

The overly confined space limits the immobile function, for it plays into the extreme category that does not interact with mobility. For any aspect that is far to the extreme without the ability of interaction with its counterpart will lose its vitality. The example of extreme mobility is a very crowded mobile space, for it loses its performative function and the interactions become individualistic and personal. By virtue of its mobility, it does not allow the resting aspect which gives rise to a performative function, such that the constituents begin to perceive the surroundings as in a state of rest and very interactive.

It can be the case that an individual may partake in that interaction, almost waiting for the crowded experience for the activation of a highly volatile interactive sentiment, for which they follow those details, gaining access that would be hard to come by in a mobile setting. However, this is not ideal, for there is always the arena to enjoin an interactive experience, and one need not entertain an extreme to experience what is readily available; as well, with the confined space which activates a highly performative function, making the experience and the interaction feel whole.

It is difficult to not think in generalities within confinement, and this would parallel the experience of extreme mobility. Thus, the experience of confinement parallels the experience of mobility prior to breaking down into the opposite extreme. As well, the experience of extreme mobility is similar to confinement before that very confinement reaches into the opposite extreme.

The realm of imitation is one of emulation, and within its parameters it is consistent with a modulation of what is reality. It isdifferent from femininity, or the opposite of masculine tendencies, in which there is a core substrate of femininity that is retained in masculinity, and it is a duo that cannot depart. Emulation, on the other hand, is a mere modulation of a substance for the integration of its sub-particles, into which there can be as many possible emulations as there are individuals integrating into those emulations, without consequence to the source or material. Femininity does not offer such, for it is constrained by masculine tendencies and, as such, is a duo that is two-part, as is all of nature, while emulation is of a different substance and serves its own critique.

Emulation's very structure relies on agreement,that one is residing in that emulation, for if they completely remove themselves from the occasion, then they become disruptive. For there is no interaction within the emulating structure as it is recognized for its realist sense and, as such, does not offer progress in its department. Furthermore, by the sociality of that emulation and imitation, it is the case that it consistently pushes the sentiment of the emulating character, such that an individual who does not agree with that reality structure will be constantly at odds between sociality and reality.

Of course, the progress of emulation is a certain dichotomy of its afforded space to offer to the real substance, for if it is believed to be wholly a substrate of reality, there is no possibility to move forward in that, as the emulating character is far different from the real substrate. All its growth and progress will be in accordance with the parameters of emulation and not with the reality substance, which, in some sense, might be the opposite. When the emulation is perceived to be wholly true, that is, when its entire substrate becomes an interaction that takes over the psyche and aligns with all sociality pertaining to reality, the default mode of character within it will not offer anything higher or more purposeful, for it already constitutes the end outcome. Because of this, there will only be a certain kind of progress afforded to the character of all emulations.

The primary character of emulation is one who is conceptually oriented, so that we could say that anybody who follows the emulation and believes it to be the only reality structure will endow a certain conceptual purview of life, in which everything is contextually oriented and structured according to systematic notions of reality. This is a character that will endow anybody who ascertains emulation to be the only reality structure, for it is emulation that takes the department of the psyche which is only of conceptual orientation. That is the locale of transition between emulation and the psyche, such that everything must fall through a conceptual overlay, and its furthest attempts will be certain levels of conceptual orientation.

Another character of emulation is its relationship to sociality, for sociality is the department of the psyche that is wholesome in its compartments, while conceptual realms are but a small component of sociality. Therefore, we could say that one who ascertains the reality of emulation to be the genuine will retain a sociality that is deferred from the normal happenstance of masculine and feminine dynamics and the regular and natural dynamics of sociality. That is, the sociality will be fairly based on the conceptual realm, so that one must be social to a point that validates that conceptual realm. However, in the sense of true sociality, there is no exchange taking place. It is merely a propagation and performance of its members to perceive such reality to be as true and validating as possible, with no nuance between those social beings other than the hierarchy in proving such validation.

A third character that manifests in emulation perceived as reality is to maintain that their reality is the only reality. Because one is attempting to ascertain something opposite of nature; to propagate a reality that does not exist, they must maintain a continuous stream of its reactions, whether it be social substrate or any other, that will retain validation on a continual basis of that reality structure as the only reality structure. We could even suggest that much of their psychic interaction revolves around seeking that very validation, leaving only a small portion devoted to the capacity to return. For this, the psyche maintains a systematic safeguard, ensuring it remains available for the unforeseen and for the deeper reality underlying intuition.

Now that we have discussed the character of emulation as perceived as the only reality, let us further understand the residence of an inhabitant within emulation while pursuing to be wholly of emulating character. It would be a continuous mockery or critique of that locale, for it manifests in the realm of validating the principle of such being a reality, and for the individual to understand otherwise would be a contrarian dynamic. Instead of one being participatory, they will become the representation and thus the critiquing member that will provide a continuous stream of interactions that prove otherwise to the system. In some sense, they take up interactions to validate the reality that they already know to exist, but because the sociality is so pertinent and follows a stream that surrounds their structure, they must maintain validation as to retain a sense of the reality that they know to be true. Instead of retaining a sociality of interactions that is wholesome, they endeavor to be a critiquing member so as to ascertain the reality structure that they know to exist.

It is because the very sociality and the structure are in a continuous process to validate their existence as true; that the individual who knows otherwise will be consistently at odds throughout their entire endeavor in that locale. In actuality, they seem to be only the critiquing individual, for they do not know any other way of approaching that sociality; especially considering that sociality is important for individuals and must be regulated and paralleled in accordance so that one perceives the reality structure to be aligned with a certain sociality. When they do not coexist, one will seek to maintain or retain a certain juncture of connection.

We may want to understand the fine line that could be accessed, for complete detachment will cause a disruption between sociality and one's understood reality, but following too earnestly will cause an entire sociality that is mere validation to uphold that premise. We can begin to dissect this dichotomy by recognizing that if interactions on a continual interval are based on exchanges that are not proper critiques, we could recognize the interactions that retain that balance. One must notice the great sacrifice at the entrance of an emulation, for whatever reality structure exists or has been associated with the psyche will be put on hold so as to follow the emulating properties. In some sense, the entrance into emulation is no different from the entrance into an educational forum, in which the rest of the psyche is put on hold to follow a contextual format, even as it appears to be an inhabitant of reality and sociality.

All engagements are contained within a certain department of the mind, so that everything is considered for the program that allows the emulation to exist. On the other hand, besides the discussion of the necessity for emulations, it is the case that during the residence in a locale of emulation it is incumbent upon the individual to retain a certain attachment to the emulating properties. This will allow the process and relationship to take effect so as to provide the provisions within that reality structure.

One cannot interact with the rubric of an emulation if they do not actualize its properties as if it were the only reality structure. The interactions will be true to the nature of the real reality structure, and everything will be in the negative connotation of what exists outside this forum. Instead, the emulation must be treated as a reality structure, even as the department of the psyche does not change; it is presumed to change to provide the availability of psyche elements and biological components that can engender a participation that will be encompassing.

If this does not occur, then there will be a depletion of contextual significance for this domain. For it is only so long that one can remain in a specific department of the psyche to interact with the simulation; at a certain point, it will seek out to remit the other parts of the psyche. But because the individual has ascertained that this is not the realistic structure of reality, all the other departments of the psyche will only partake to recognize that recognition. This will cause a disruption of consciousness.

Consciousness is completely entrenched in reality structures; some emulated and others of the realistic nature of substance, but in the case where the other departments of the psyche are not allowed to actualize this locale, consciousness is not allowed into its domain. The entire sociality will interact to recognize that provision, that principle of the very fact that the simulation is not a reality structure, only to further entrench the psyche away from conscious rumination. There is no ability to structurally reattach to the reality structure external to this realm, for the sociality is in a continual stream of validating this simulation as the reality structure. Whatever structural or memorable input the individual offers will not do much to provide the psyche with conscious stimulation.

We may wonder why every individual under the rubric of this emulation will not be reposed from the contextual department of the psyche, for even if it is actualized to presume the entirety of the psyche, it is the case that it is but a fabrication, for reality emanates from that department of the psyche. However, reality on the ground is not as perfect as reality as a presumption of the psyche. From the psyche's perspective, it is assumed that this is the reality structure, even as we study the psyche components and recognize that it is only the part, the department of contextual database, that allows for the simulation to take effect.

In some sense, the psyche knows or must follow the rules of reality to provide stimulation of the emulation only from this department of the psyche. But because of a preconception, other avenues are taken to access the utility of the rest of the psyche and the biological system. It is as if one is hacking the system while still providing the emulating factor rom a specific department of the psyche. An individual has the ability to hack the psyche or biological system by the variability of actualizing whatever they see fit to actualize, even if it does not parallel reality.

The process of actualization is a process in which one overrides the reality of the structure of the psyche, providing a consistent stream of functionality for the emulating parameters. Thus, experienced personhood would be that the emulation is the full embodiment of personhood and psyche parameters, even as the department of all its substrates is but the contextual domain. Only for so long can one follow this procedure of actualizing a reality that does not parallel the existence of the psyche and the process of its parameters; thus, one must continuously validate their premise and justify its system.

In some sense, they must enter into a contextual realm on a continual basis and proceed to reaffirm and attach to the emulating system, which then must be actualized in the department of actualization to override and access the entire biological system. We can notice this on a regular basis, for in the early mornings in these emulating locales, there will be a contextual oversight in which every individual will almost reattach to the matrix. Once the contextual realm is sufficient, there will be a natural depletion of its substance so as to reaffirm to the rest of the psyche.

At that interval, namely in the afternoon or late afternoon, the psyche has a choice: either to dismember the emulation and thus follow a sequence of events that will prove fruitful in that endeavor, or to actualize that locality for the provision of the rest of the biological system. Later in the day, at some time in the evening, the biological system will recognize or will be depleted from the lack of parallel between the psyche's reality and the process of actualization, at which point it will seek out a reality other than its proposed actualization. In that case, the actualization becomes a non-contender, and rather the individual is once again in pursuit of the reality which the psyche demands and which follows its parameters.

In most cases, the individual will not follow that process and instead will repress the material, attempting to actualize to a further degree, to the point where the actualization is of less material and will not allow access to the amenities of the biological system. This can lead to a perpetual decline in which even an attempted actualization will not have the effect of allowing access to the system, for there is a heightened disparity between the psycho-process and the individual's presumptions. In this case, the individual must retain a stronger contextual overlord of the system to ascertain the emulation and thus begin a process of sociality that assists in that validation.

For when we are able to entertain a sociality that provides a connection to that validation, what becomes of the final product is a very helpful assistant. That reality is constructed, in some sense, by sociality; so, if we can perform a sociality that follows that sequence, then we have an advantage over reality, even the reality of the psyche system during its process.

We can notice those individuals who perceive a certain emulation with such veneration to be also those who follow a stronger contextual premise to ascertain that department of the psyche. For them, they utilize that department of the psyche as if it must sequence the entire psyche, and thus follow a sequence of perpetual manipulation between how the psyche functions and their propositions.

Once the emulation is discounted, the reality of the psyche will take effect, and it will recognize its process under its realistic parameters. The process of discounting takes effect when, after a certain actualization is in method, the individual proceeds to recognize the validity of that actualization to its realistic standards. The difficulty of discounting an emulation is that upon the end of sequence one is met with a dearth of consciousness, for they are surrounded by a sociality that still sustains that validation of reality. Secondly, there is an inherent loss of conscious experience, for whatever was perceived as consciousness has been pulled out and recognized as fabrication.

Whatever dormant consciousness belongs to a structural sustainment of the realistic state of consciousness, which in an emulation ceremony does not exist, pertains to a sociality that spends most of its interactions disrupting that structural connection from its manifestation. In the event of emulations that still sustain a structural connection to the overarching reality of conscious information, there is always a standard from which one cannot disengage, for it is the reality through which the psyche processes its system. Thus, discounting locales, one cannot discount the realistic state of consciousness as it is. When one attempts to do such in the midst of realistic consciousness, they find themselves discounting of personhood itself,to the sense of a personality disruption.

To discount the reality structure, one needs to recognize what is toward the realistic state of the psyche. When discounting moves something closer to the realistic state of the psyche, more questioning is necessary; while when further away, the discounting is rather obvious and requires more immediate attention to its validation. It would not suffice to merely consider discounting reality structures, for then one would be privy only to the reality structure of the realistic state of the psyche and thus without validation of partitions that are necessary for the progress of the psyche.

Meaning to say, even if there is a true nature to the psyche, it requires validation, emulation, and actualization of partitions that deserve recognition as their distinct domain, with domesticity within its departments. For domestication is the very aspect of providing actualization to departments of the psyche that do not parallel the completeness and wholesome nature of the psyche. However, we find more prevalence of the failure to disrupt and discount reality structures that do not parallel the realistic state of the psyche than individuals who find difficulty in the validation and progress of subdomains that deserve actualization despite their disparity to the realistic state of the psyche.

It is also the case that one can presume residence to the realistic state of the psyche without negotiation of these domains, for there is no disruption between themselves and reality, only that their connection to conscious material is losing its substantial weight, for there is no domain through which to perceive its structure other than itself. Thus, we require contextual demands that oppose, coincide, and parallel one another to provide that weighted understanding of these domains. Still, the slim nature of the reality of existence is a practice of substantial continuation, while reality structures that do not parallel existence will always be at the expense of existence and will shape personhood accordingly.

Relation as Means of Understanding

The matter of fact of life bearing is that the succession of one's endeavors has won or lost to the existential reality of the prior models and stages. This cannot be cumbersome if one remembers those elements when needed for non-existential matters. In most cases, a mere remembrance or recognition of the progress of growth and the evolution of standards will be enough to enable the widespread aspects of the individual to deal and tend to the layers of their nuance.

This change is when there is an existential necessity that will only be endeavored through existential awareness, which is beyond the state of understanding and is the embodiment of that emulation. For instance, there is no ability in one to recognize the state of needing a home unless one is endeavoring in the experience of being lost to a home ground. Even if one has the memory, it would not be enough, for there is no existential access and it would not be as if one is in the state of necessity as they were in that preoccupation.

It is the case that reality is not that structure, and to convince the psyche otherwise is a lost endeavor in terms of conceptual awareness. However, in terms of emulation, things change, for at least for an interval, there is an existential awareness. Though it is conceptually oriented, it is perceived through some existential forum. It is like one who is stuck in the emulation and perceives the reality to be true; as for the properties of providing an existential reality, it has done its job, although it is made aware through a part of the psyche that is not existentially bound, such that it will not be an existential continuity of their development.

While this is enough, for one just needs to endeavor toward the existential makeup for the awareness properties. It is not for the sake of residing in that setting, for then they would not need to negate their entire structure henceforth in order to provide that trueness at the psyche level.

For instance, in the case of the loss of home or the experience of such in an existential manner, one can approach the endeavor in two different manners. One would be to take on a material manifestation of what it would mean to lose a home; to disembark and shred away from that comfort to a point where there is almost no distinction between their experience and the experience of a loss of home, despite it being prevalent in the background.

The same can be said for money, it is not the fact of having or not having as perceived in the materialistic perspective, but rather in the attachment to its substrate. If one were to endeavor, despite having such in the background, into a local experience that would be at a loss, or if they entered into an environment where it would not matter much, then they would be able to reinvent that existential experience so as to continue the foreboding of the wholesome personhood that makes decisions according to both those models, one of insecurity and one of security.

For the decisions that are made based on security will be without the recognition of those necessities, especially the existential necessity, such that it would automatically be a choice in the wrong departments, for it is coming from mere access rather than mere necessity. Therefore, one must engage in the model of necessity because that is the only realm that would progress the choices forward, and anything from a place of stability or security will disrupt what is true.

Additionally, anything that is chosen from security and stability will be engaged from that stage even if it does meet and converge at the interval of necessity, meaning if we were to remove the stability layer, still that would be the choice activity, for the psyche would not receive it as such, but rather as the ready-presumed reality that will exist and does not need fulfillment or validation in its continuity.

In some sense, there is no fulfillment occurring once there is stability; it is just a mere foundation of the already-sequenced event of accepting security and stability. Such that every social thing would necessitate continuing the modulation of what it would mean to be a necessity, despite their prevalence in the state of security and stability.

Almost as if to say that the state of security and stability is of no real necessity for the social being because it automatically will deviate toward a worse-off choice experience. However, the provision of stability and security is that it grants the availability of psyche movements that do not correlate to necessity, that we could even have this conversation, because we have access to a state of security and stability. For if we merely protracted from necessity then nothing that is removed from the state of necessity would be able to be accessed, let alone discussed, dissected, thought, or experienced in dialogue.

Section Four: On the Exchange Between Security and Necessity: Hosting, Empathy, and the Reclamation of Existential Awareness

For the second approach, instead of experiencing the existential state through parameters that disallow the security and stability that would be prevalent, even if there is a background of that, if it is not existentially experienced at the moment, it would be a case of insecurity. This approach takes the dynamic exchange of those who are in the state of necessity so as to formulate a bond that would allow them to converge into a state of security while they offer themselves as the existential state of insecurity.

For instance, in the case of hosting, when one has a home and takes in a stranger, or someone who lacks the security of a home blanket, one gains access to the existential state of someone without a home. While the host provides security for the moment, they are unable to utilize all the provisions that such security affords for psyche movement. However, in this approach, it is easy to deviate, as it could be perceived as a form of generosity or reciprocity from the upper echelons to the lower echelons, rather than the dynamic exchange that is truly necessary.

What would occur is that, instead of the natural dynamical exchange, one would revalidate their state of security and experience a certain guilt so as to spread their availability of security to those who do not have it. Although this seems altruistic, it does not provide the provision, as we discussed, for there is no existential experience of what it is like to be on the other side. We must perceive generosity not as a case of fighting what others do not have but rather as obtaining what one does not have, which is the case of the modulation of necessity.

In fact, it would be more accessible if one gained empathetic experience of the other side, not so much for the giving and taking, but rather just for empathy's sake, so as to experience that existential state. The mere giving of generosity is an exchange, a market exchange actually, that allows something more substantial to take place, as in any exchange of material goods.

We could almost be apathetic toward this approach because there are so many ways it goes wrong and fails to provide the dynamic change. We might instead prefer to depart from states of security in order to gain the provisions of insecurity and necessity. Yet we do understand that, in the case of hosting, it would be fairly beneficial for a family body to gain the entrance of those without, so that the exchange will be almost inevitable if the dialogue is prolonged and protracted for a certain duration of time.

It would be the same if one were to become friends with those in a state of necessity, so that in that endeavor, at some point, one will gain access to that existential state. This is why hosting is more beneficial for an awareness of necessity than embarking on a departure from the security of the home blanket. Because a prolonged period of dynamical exchanges, especially with wholesome dialogue, will bring the inevitable awareness that one side has security and the other has lacks such; so that appreciation on one side and recognition on the other complete the dynamical exchange.

In the case of generosity and currency value, it is the other way around, because there is a lack of dialogue or social transferring in the experience of that exchange. In fact, it is socially unacceptable to prolong that exchange, so that if one were to attempt the exchange in proper proportions, they would need to reside among those of necessity, which can become problematic for the very fact that they live in those domains and ruminate a certain value structure based on necessity.

That value structure is wholly different from one which is at a loss of a homebody, so that one who allows the hosting into their homebody of individuals that do not have, without the recognition of the costs of being exposed to the moral structure of those lacking that, will get it wrong. Because the loss of a homebody or lack of stability is not the cause of a decrepit value system in its original sum but rather in its nuanced layers, it would not provide a deficiency in the hosting structure.

In cases of monetary necessity, the value structure is often degraded for the fully formed social being. Those who recall such a state know it is profoundly unstable for trust in the collective of social beings and for the moment-to-moment perception of reality and others in terms of their consumptive nature, especially as psyche movements unrelated to immediate provision are lost, reducing one to little more than an animal of the hunt.

If one remembers the loss of a homebody or the lack thereof, it is usually of a more subtle value system, in which there is a loss of central themes and groundedness and other such forms, but almost as if the social structure is not detestable and could be praised for its individuality that is allowed unlimited expression.

We conclude, for one, that the approach is more prevalent to be the dynamic exchange, and for the other, the approach to be one's individual endeavors, because of the fact that the dynamic exchange, when done in its fully developed mental state, is costly to the human expanse.

We will touch on a few further examples in understanding the differences between these two approaches.

The instance of emulating being a child, so that every adult would be at a loss for that existential experience, may make us wonder why there is a need for existential awareness rather than mere memory. This is because the existential state of childhood is necessary for adulthood. When such innocence is lost and growth evolves, adulthood becomes stagnant in its form, since it rests solely on that evolution. Without access to the existential dimension, adulthood merely represents its own image and cannot continue unless it emulates the very instances of childhood.

This is not a necessity in the same way as the other two examples, but it remains significant in the structure of the social being. In this case, the social exchange between child and adult may be more prevalent as a chosen activity, as both would benefit without degrading the other's moral system. It becomes a wholesome endeavor, where each side contributes to the forum, and the dialogue is perfected for the growth of both.

While the other choice, of approaching an emulation of being a child with the departure of adulthood so that the activity would be on par with childhood it would be destructive to the sense of adulthood.

Differing from the first two instances, where the expense is not of psychological or conceptual growth but rather materialistic growth, one can always remove the extra material to emulate a model that is without such, which is very different from one that removes the conceptual expanse for the gain of a memory and its actualization.

There would be a momentary loss of adulthood when the endeavor is sought, and we may find it common that those who follow this path almost become childlike in their adulthood, so that the seriousness that is necessary is lost and they need to experience maturity once again. This is not to say that the emulation of preliminary conceptual modalities is always faulty, but it is the recognition that it does provide the mistakes which could occur and disrupt conceptual growth, reverting and regressing the entire system back to those former states.

Another instance of this exchange is masculinity and femininity, for all individuals begin their evolution from the feminine standpoint and either fall to a more nuanced stance in that femininity or protract and become a masculine figure. However, it is always the case that all social beings need to experience the existential case of the feminine disposition, whether it is the expanse of the nuances of femininity that need to experience the preliminary state of femininity, or it is the masculine disposition which must reconsider the existential state of femininity that lurks behind their substructure.

In this case, the noticeable answer stands, for instead of embarking on a journey in which one must reimagine themselves in a feminine or preliminary feminine disposition, they can easily provide a social exchange for that endeavor, especially considering that the entire sexual process is based on that very exchange, such that the social substructure is oriented to provide those provisions.

The exchange is alongside romance, marriage, and sexual endeavors. In all such cases, it is the ability of one disposition to gain the existential state of the other in its fully formed aspects. We may want to understand the benefit of femininity in gaining the exchange of masculinity, and that is for the potential of femininity and its more nuanced layers that reach out and attract the nuances and receptivity of masculinity.

Either way, the exchange is necessary, whether for potential or for existential remembrance, but without existential awareness, one would be at a loss of oneself, such that it becomes less relatable and more prevalent to presume the masculine state is the original one.

Section Five: Between Simulation and Reality

A general reality can become a simulation through various methods, while a simulation can become a general reality through other methods. The method of a general reality becoming a simulation is through the disassembly of its parameters that formulate it as a reality. These parameters can be found in the manner in which it intersects with the amalgamation of consciousness through the various figures who lead that query.

As we noted in other works, in the three layers of a structured environment, there is going to be that layer of consciousness in which, despite whatever the political prevalence or representation of that leadership, there is the underlying consciousness flow and its development that is most deserving of recognition. For it is this reality that leads the parameters of the system.

When there is a disparity between the conscious continuum and the structured environment, then the experienced state of that infrastructure is simulated. When we understand a simulation, we recognize that it does not follow the rules of reality. That ability to unfollow reality for whatever sake is only made available by the subjugation of a consciousness continuum into its midst. When that consciousness continuum begins to manifest at a rate that affects sociality, then the simulation is lost, and it is rather considered a reality.

For example, under a digital simulation, one will be propelled to reality if consciousness permeates that habitat, wherever that manifests. The only manner to maintain that simulation is by diverting conscious continuums so that there is a separation to allow for the simulation to take effect. Therefore, when a general reality diverts from its conscious underpinning through the separation of its basic infrastructural habitat, it becomes a simulation. Even if the consciousness continuum can be found in the depths of that reality; just as a simulation, if studied properly, would be found to be engaging with the conscious continuum because it is not actualized and manifested in an agreeable manner with the infrastructure itself, the environment enters into a simulation until it arises again.

The same can be said for a conscious continuum that overtakes an environment, to which, instead of the alternative of disparity, it leads the way for progress while the infrastructure lags in its implementation of the flow. The outcome is the same, where the environment will become a simulation because of the effect of a disparity between itself and its potential. Instead of the conscious continuum providing much-needed vitality in the platform of what is, the potential of consciousness stretches so that its actualization is an impossible feat, thereby causing the environment to become a simulation, not by its lack of conscious flow but by its unattainable convergence with it.

The direct relationship between an environment and its conscious flow is the single most determinant for the resolution of it being a simulation or a general reality. Because there is structural dependence, any locale outside of the central rumination will be governed by this clause, but as well, by the dependency itself. Even if a dependent locale does relegate between its consciousness flow and actualized environment, it will still receive the rumination of the central locale in which it maintains a disparity between those two proponents.

Meaning to say, a locale can govern only to the advantage of itself until it must accept the ruminating effect and its dependency upon the lineage of the central locale. In fact, it is this very offset that causes even further disruptions, because if the central locale has become a simulation and all its rumination is thus part of that process, then the dependencies which make for the closure of that disparity will cause them to be an apportioned reality that is higher than their dependency.

A formulated general reality that relies upon a simulated reality will only enlarge the disparity of the simulation. For example, in the digital simulation, if we were to effect a general reality from the simulation, whatever developments they make to converge the conscious stream and structured reality, it will still service the general simulation. The characters' life that is enjoined in such a reality framework, which cannot be said for the simulation and the world around it, meaning to say that there is less disparity between the characters' life and the simulated reality than there is between the simulation and the world around it, will cause the simulation to become more separate from the world around it.

Another concrete example would be film, which is a simulated reality that is at any time in disparity with the real world. However, if we were to have a character in the film become self-aware so that they begin to believe in the reality of their character environment; and if this is done in a manner where there is less disparity between the character and the film environment than between the film and the real world, then it would only increase the film's overall disparity, as the character serves the simulating effect.

We can even question the prospect of a character engaging in self-aware experiences as if they were non-simulating when the entire environment is a clear indication of a simulated backdrop. Why would the character of a film become more deeply attached to the film's environment than the film itself is to the external realm? The only possible explanation is that the character operates within a system of governance that excludes the backdrop of the realistic environment from which they originate.

Instead, the effect of their determinant nature, of performing themselves as a reality within a simulation, will only have their perceived reality become more attached to the simulation as opposed to the external realm. As well, the simulation will become more entrenched in the realistic framework of its environment because the character has taken the role more seriously.

Any attempt at tailoring the simulation with the external realm will fall short because it is being further enacted within its system. Similar to the manner in which a digital simulation that advances is the replication of characters who are personified to a degree in which the simulation loses its availability for external engagement, having the perfect effect of simulation but at the expense of its entire objective: that of interacting with the external realm.

Although locales can be treated for their competency in their departments, it may be that every step of competency is an actual reversal of such, because they are not aware of their dependencies, which do not share that level of competency. This is the manner of utopian locales or organizations, in which their competency is not shared by their dependent locales, so that every stride of progress is retro-progress, because it only enlarges the disparity toward their dependency and its convergence with consciousness.

This is why we often find resentment towards institutional locales from utopian environments, as they are subconsciously aware that their hopeful stride has only deepened their dependency upon the central locale. Their expansion in their futile locale is the expansion of the disparity of their dependence on its convergence, which in turn has them become less available for independence from that dependency. The character expansion only makes them more entrenched in the simulation instead of assuming themselves to be a progressive figure in that environment. As well, the character expansion also creates more division between the external realm and the simulation.

Chapter Five: Representation and Simulation

Section One: The Dynamics of Immersive and Structured Gaming

The following example illustrates how contemporary gaming environments extend imitation beyond social modeling into full-bodied simulation, offering a lens through which to examine immersion, representation, and the limits of identity. We have an understanding that if one is to interact with what we call structured simulation-based games, the objective is more of a coordinated effort between user and game such that they are building alongside it. The purpose and objective of the game is to gain a simulated experience so that the individual may move about in an interactive manner and thus come to identifications within themselves alongside the platform they are simulating.

The other possibility is an immersive experience, almost like a darkened cinematic experience, where one becomes the user themselves, like a sensory or psychological first-person experience. It is mostly about gaining cinematic entertainment at a higher level rather than focusing on the process of the game or the interaction itself. It is a further attempt at attaining territory within the simulatory aspect of gaming so that one becomes absorbed in that realm, not so much for interaction, because then they would have to align themselves and remain in constant communion between themselves and the game, but rather to be the game itself.

And this is where motor skills takes part because there has to be some element that stimulates the user in their own immersion through interaction. In order for true immersion to happen, one requires their physical body to perform the deeds that would allow such; any form of conceptual output would not be enough. We need to find something in the physical form that generates that level of simulation.

Thus, motor skills become the primary target, almost like a forceful necessity, introducing competition rather than regular interaction. Since there is no actual possibility of physically entertaining the notion of a game, for it is separate from the real world and only a simulation, one is at odds with how to perform this immersion. What comes about is this concoction between the highest form of conceptual interests, thus the most politically entertaining or traumatic notions of experience, hence warfare and its various forms, and the notion of motor skills, which puts one in a position where their ability to perform with their body becomes the fortification of the game.

This is why such games heavily lean on shooting aspects, as they serve as a dramatic reincarnation of the most brutal aspects of humankind, or more so, the most politically relevant or immersive childhood experiences. A gun, for instance, stands in a room like nothing else because of its power upon society and between people. Thus, it is the gun, or warfare in general, where the carnage of battle becomes the most politically stimulating theme, whether for a child or an adult, because of its relevance. It thus becomes a marker for structured interaction.

Chapter Six: Representation and Social Manifestation

A representation can be considered distinctive and secluded from the entire spectrum of consciousness and is reliant upon a consciousness head, which can be found through memory or through current sociality. A conscious head, by default, relies upon sociality, not infrastructure itself. We could imagine a dystopian realm; an infrastructure that represents consciousness but lacks sociality, so that it is completely reliant on memory, not concurrent sociality.

When infrastructure solely applies the added effect of that representation to align itself genuinely with sociality, symbiotic relationships form. If we fail to contain the admixture of infrastructure and sociality, the attempted representations will not reflect the environmental context, causing the infrastructure to disrupt the complete representation and rebound. It will rebound because the infrastructure will offer the reverse representation of the attempted sociality, disrupting conscious fluidity or ascendency. The infrastructure will then present its polar opposite, forcing the individual to reflect back onto themselves via their perceptual realm against the very attempted representation.

For example, if one attempts to represent themselves as a certain persona, as where the infrastructure is not aligned with such, it will reflect against the notion of that persona. The infrastructure will not reinforce the representation but instead reflect the shadow of that very attempted rapresentation, leaving the individual as not only without a representation, but a proclaimed cautionary tale of its ideation.

Novel items, whether by representation of being or substrate, will generate sentimental weight within the preliminary layers of one's psyche. As the novel item or animation proceeds along its sequence, so that it is further promoted to being an acquisition of novel sentiment, it becomes the realization of, and the manner in which it proposes, how one is built upon layers of consciousness that are foundational. It seems, to the contrary, that something innovative or novel would exemplify progress by disrupting itself from its history; but the opposite is true. The constant relayment of experience, and the observation of how novel sentiment passes along its growth stages, gives rise to the historical sentiments of those who interact with it; not for the intrinsic history in the substrate itself, but as a reflection of once-concurrent foundational elements.

We can notice this in the common fixation on acquiescing to a novel notion or sentiment at a very preliminary stage and purposefully ignoring its continuance as it progresses along its sequence, so that it never has the opportunity to represent itself as more than just the novel beginning. Rather, it is sequestered from making a case for foundational elements or one's reflection. This is seen clearly in the societal tendency to give the greatest reverence to infants in close approximation to birth, and the steep decline in such revere as the child progresses into toddlerhood. The infant stage exemplifies one's preliminary stages of development, while the continuation of growth does no such thing, and in fact credits a stronghold of progress without attachment to the foundational layers that led to it.

The general decline of reverence of the representation of a child toward adulthood is most accurately seen in how they exemplify preliminary layers in one's reflection, and the more so they do, the less reverence they receive. The reason for this mediated concern for preliminary layers as representation is that, in some accurate sense, it is not the founded exemplification of a being, but rather its preliminary possibility, or the potential that brings forth being, rather than being itself. However, it is also the case that such exemplification reveals the vulnerability of maturity, in that it acknowledges the necessity of following a sequence of prior stages of consciousness, and that, in neglecting this, one becomes forlorn in their current development. This dichotomy causes both extremes: on one hand, a logical foundation for disregarding preliminary layers as representation due to their degeneration of being, and on the other, a tendency to use the dissonance of such representation to proclaim a fervent unnecessity for foundational integration.

Cultural differences often arise when there is a temporal or spatial gap between an event and its representation. To the contrary, when there is spatial or temporal proximity, that is, when the thing itself is as animated to the perceptual realm as possible, there are mitigated cultural gaps. There is something pressing in the perceptual agreement that something is alive, or as close in proximity to the perceptual senses as possible; that cannot be attributed to cultural relevance. Although there is a rather pressing notoriety to the cultural gap in proportion to perceptual distance, one which cannot be attributed to the cultural difference itself but rather to a psychological experience that happens to correlate with a cultural difference. The only matter that offers correlation is that different geographic regions usually develop distinct cultural identities.

Menninghaus et al. (2017) argue that representations inherently create psychological and cultural distancing, as they provide only an indirect and incomplete exposure to the original context. With that assumption, the context is approved to be in milieu with the assumed nature of the given art form as received by the common individual, although such context could vary to a point where there is no distance. But it is not directly linked.xxv

The matter of fact that there is a perceptual agreement is the area of concern for us. One can easily access a perceptual agreement in any arena or in any art form. As noted by Menninghaus, children will perceive without a spatial or temporal difference. This is why there is an intuitive sense for parental figures to guide children's away from these art forms, especially pornography or extreme violence, for they, that is the children, will not be able to differentiate that distance. However, as the mature form develops, there is no reason that one would not be able to access that very infantile state of blurring the lines between perceptual inference and fabricated forms of entertainment. Yet, the senses will be attuned to the difference between what is perceptually linked and what is formatted for perceptual input, because that is the very demarcation of individuality versus the perceptual world.

In the case of a traumatic event, for example, one loses the distinction between the substance of the trauma and their own perception; thus, they become intertwined with the experience as if they are the experience in its full sense, so that it can no longer be considered a simple external inference but rather an environment of that situation. The reason that only a traumatic event would entice such a loss of distinction is because one verifiably becomes attached to the experience through the mediums of its proposing substance that, in a regular case, would not be entertained. Although we could also argue that with enough occurrences of trauma, or the blurring of lines between perception and experience, one would become unified with external reality, like the antiquated human being, and therefore would not experience the notion or ability of experiencing trauma, because their internal manifestation or psyche has become part and parcel with external reality.

When there is a notion of disruption in the external world, it is felt in the psyche, and when there is a disruption in the psyche, it is felt in the external world, so that it becomes so unified that, in a way, one would not be fooled into psyche meanderings, becoming more and more aligned with perceptual reality as it were. However, when perceptual reality takes a downward spiral, or if a simple enlistment of an emotionative experience occurs, it will be the full manifestation of revenge, resentment, or anger without any mitigation, because it is unified without a distinction.

In a way, the mammalian brain activates in this regard: a threat is considered a threat on their life because there is no matter of distinction between what the psyche experience is, a foreboding threat, and what the external reality is presenting. On the extreme side, the fully developed and formed human being has a conscious layer that distinguishes, in constant motion, that differentiation, so that internal mechanisms of emotion and experience are not translated into the external world and vice versa. However, the middle ground, when one either deviates from the fully scoped conscious experience or when one is developing from the mammalian mind to become part of the conscious experience, creates a complication between what is a derivative of the psyche experience and what is a manifestation of external reality.

For at times, a threat can simply be an existential dread of the moment, having nothing to do with the relation between perception and reality. At other times, it is perception itself that is foreboding a semblance of disruption, where the psyche is simply activating its mechanisms in response to that. Because of this, every case would have a mixture of both, so that a constant mediation is required to notice how much of the emotion or experience is from perceptual reality and how much is based on one's existential experience through the recreation of the psyche material and distinct from external reality.

For sure, there is an element in which spatial or temporal distance creates a gap because culture is defined by location and time, but that is not always the case. For instance, when the current culture embodies ancient culture there is a cultural gap but not necessarily a temporal or spatial one. Or otherwise, the other way around, where there is no cultural gap because there is a synthesis of that architecture, but there is a temporal and spatial gap because the source of that architecture is engineered by the former culture.

Menninghaus et al. (2017) claim that "representations support only distanced, indirect, and, in comparison to their real antecedents, incomplete exposure" (p. 7). However, this argument does not account for instances where cultural transmission mitigates these distances. Cultural gaps are not simply a byproduct of time and space; they are shaped by how societies choose to engage with their past. By preserving, reviving, and integrating historical and foreign influences, cultures actively counteract the distancing effects that Menninghaus et al. describe.xxvi

Temporal and spatial distances can often lead to cultural differences, but it is not a one-to-one relationship. Consider Roman architecture in New York City. Although the design originates from ancient Roman engineering (a clear temporal and spatial gap), its integration into New York's urban landscape creates a hybrid cultural space. Here, the cultural gap is mitigated by a shared appreciation for classical aesthetics, even though the original context is quite different.

Moreover, cultural synthesis can occur in such a way that temporal distance does not translate into cultural distance. Many societies actively preserve and incorporate elements of their past, maintaining a strong connection to historical influences. A prime example is the preservation of Shakespearean language and literature in modern Anglo-Saxon cultures. Although centuries have passed, the continued study, adaptation, and performance of Shakespeare's works show that cultural continuity can exist despite significant temporal separation.

Conversely, you might have situations where a society adopts or synthesizes ancient elements so thoroughly that the temporal gap feels minimal culturally, even though the source is ancient. In this case, architecture carries both its Roman heritage and its new cultural meaning. The key point is that while temporal and spatial differences can contribute to cultural gaps, factors like cultural synthesis, continuity, or deliberate reinterpretation can bridge that gap.

This argument challenges the research that assumes cultural gaps emerge naturally due to shifts in time or space. The research suggests that representations support only distanced, indirect, and, in comparison to their real antecedents, incomplete exposure, and that this should, in principle, work in favor of a psychologically more distanced response. However, this does not hold in cases where cultural continuity exists; where societies deliberately preserve or re-contextualize past cultures within their present. The cultural continuity in architectural appreciation prevents a full cultural gap from forming with Roman Architecture.

Therefore, the idea that a cultural gap is automatic due to spatial or temporal differences is not absolute. While shifts in time and place often bring about cultural distinctions, there are cases where cultures sustain elements of the past or integrate foreign influences seamlessly, negating the expected gap. Cultural transmission, preservation, and adaptation are forces that complicate the notion that time and space alone determine cultural divergence.

Clothing would be the most essential item to a higher life form succeeding in biological necessities, and likely the primary item to bring along during a change of location. If we are to understand representations, we must understand clothing. The first aspect of clothing is that it is engineered for the body, so much so that it becomes synonymous with the body, serving as its primary representation.

Although the body in its naked state retains a certain representational quality, as previously discussed, it is only when posturing is involved that the body becomes a deliberate representation. An unanimated body is typically not considered postured, and therefore not representational. However, an unanimated body that is clothed still retains a degree of representation, thus proving that clothing is the primary representation of the body, even to the extent that the body itself may be considered less primary in some contexts.

If we were to consider animation as a representation, we would then need to identify the source it represents, yet we would be unable to construct a substantial theory. We might reach metaphysical theories, but these are only representations of animation. One could proclaim that animation is an element that has no further source to correlate with it. While theoretical and religious frameworks may attempt to understand animation, the very fact that they must rely on theory already implies an agreement: that animation is the source from which theories themselves emerge.

Because clothing is one of, if not the most primary, representations of animation, it would be the most primary representation to exist. Nothing other than maybe the body itself, or a form of posturing the body, would contest that space. Therefore, all representations will be dependent in some form upon clothing or its source of animating spirit. The animating spirit is the source and does not represent itself, but there are elements that can represent an animating spirit and consequently are akin to clothing. While clothing provides ample representation for the animation of the corporeal structure, it begins to lose traction from animating spirits that emanate from the psyche via consciousness, or knowledge and wisdom. Clothing is perfected to represent the body formation, and in fact is in conflict with a representation of psyche elements because it would be at the expense of the wholeness of the body.

However, representations that take up the spatial requirements of the animating spirit are vast and encompass most of contemporary representations. Yet, it is these representations that do not require a cemented form because they are representing something that is not physically formed to the same extent as the body. The parameters of clothing are both limited, definable, and necessarily tangible, while psyche representations do not need to be limited, nor are they necessarily definable. They can move between items quickly and do not require physical means or space, as a cup can remind one of major ideas or eras of life. In fact, we usually find that through access to means, one utilizes less of the possibility of representing intrinsic aspects of their psyche and instead seek out representations of consciousness itself.

This leads to the third category of representations, those that represent consciousness instead of merely psyche elements. Consciousness is defined by what is currently cogitating, and many will find that they retain representations of consciousness that are dated, only to compel them to continue that consciousness flow despite the change of environment. This is a problem with architecture, for it is based on scheming and implementing over an expanse of time, time which does change against whatever consciousness is being represented. This is why the most pertinent architecture covers themes that take part in a vastness of culture, to which it would require a major change of civilization for that relevance to depart.

Chapter Seven: Practical Applications

A symbol is both an invitation towards entry and the ambivalent nature of its doubting last sentiment before the succeeding events, where the symbol and its symbolic framework concede to their general process. By having these two elements correspond to each other, it is a matter of interaction that outlays its process. The viewer of the symbol is as important as the discussion in regard to the symbol itself because of this ambivalence. When we do not consider the context of the symbol pertaining to the framework as elicited by the individual, we automatically place a subconscious equivalent of such, according to our associations.

We would not do to engage with a symbol by mere fact as being another object, for at least from the understanding that there is a social agreement would constitute that we need to participate, as would if we notice a social upheaval near us. This is an existential demand, built by our social criteria henceforth, where even in the case which an indigenous population brings about their symbolic forms, by the mere fact that we see other social beings bear to a constitution of their framework corresponding to a symbol would have us interact accordingly. Although we may be of little interest in the entire framework to which it corresponds, for instance a flag of a state where no significant attachment emerges, still by the emblem carried in a social criterion would have one participate in the sociality as if it were their own.

In the case which there is little correlation, or if the emblem is arbitrary to existing sociality, then it would not constitute a symbol for it does not include a complexity of information but rather is constructed by sheer necessity. An example of this is a company that does not intersect with general sociality, but nonetheless is part of the economic forum, to which it would necessitate a sort of symbol to correspond to the entirety of the company. By the fact that it does not preclude a divestment of sociality, to which the emblem thus contains, it will not be considered a genuine symbol, and thus little to no participation at that end. We do not perceive the symbol to contain much information, and rather that it is felt coerced in its construction, without a social backing.

To follow the example further, we may place the symbolic framework serving as the symbol for indigenous populations, or the deep subconscious as serving the anthropologic history to which there is some laden anchor through the lineage, especially if civilization is a more complex form of that. Suffice to say that as long as social organization is correlated, then the symbol will have some existential participation, to which we decide the framework, or it would be decided by the subconscious, in its agreement that something must be provided.

A great illustration is the stop sign, and practically any signage that is not directional would constitute a symbol, demanding participation beyond the regulation of the symbol itself. For the stop sign does, in fact, invite participation into the procedure that enables interaction between viewer and signage. But only by the final analysis is the stop sign determined to have the individual depart by halting in that participation. It is this ambivalent nature that expresses itself in such signage, for it attempts to correlate to eventual separation; and with this, one is existentially perplexed.

Symbols, then, invite the participant to exemplify the amplitude of their correlation to a proceeding substantiation of consciousness or the source material that a framework proceeds henceforth. In this way, not all frameworks can provide a symbol, either because they are so oriented in their substructure that their symbolic nature is unnecessary, or they lack a form of complexity to which a symbol is not needed.

A family, for example, usually does not require a symbol for the family structure, to which it is believed to either be without complexity, or is so inclusive to its substrate that any emblem would dilute it. It is usually the former, where the family, although most significant in many other arenas, in the form of complexity that would constitute a need for such generalization, there is none. The family is dependent on the political form, so that in all cases, they interact based on a larger framework, and would not require their own form of institution, and by that, we have explained the difference between institution and domestication.

To proceed from the earlier example, there is no requisite for a symbol to exemplify that a road is in fact a road. It is the case that the symbol is necessary at an intersection, where it is unclear to the procedural behavior reflecting the participation of infrastructural rules based on political processes. It is the political criteria that are the earliest procedures providing signage for road infrastructure because of the regulation of that process.

We could view the symbol as communication in this context, but it would dilute its significance. Instead of providing communication that would be language or facial expression, we have a criterion in which the amount of communication or the complexity of communication itself is so simple that the final procedure is to provide a symbol. We provide a form of signage by road infrastructure because there is no way to exemplify to the public, through communication, the distinctive behaviors and proper usage of roads. The point where communication breaks down is thus the symbol itself, which is different from, for example, a traffic light.

The reason the traffic light is different and does not constitute itself as a symbol is because it is, in fact, acting as an officer, providing distinct direction. It is not left up to decision-making or the availability of individual interaction. Instead, it operates without participation other than the awareness that its color-coded aspects represent the gestures of distinctive officers. The traffic light serves as a direct communication from political authorities to the road, without the need for interaction, in contrast to regular road signage.

The difference then is that road signage or symbols simplify the interaction between fewer elements so that the eventual outcome conveys the complexity that was unable to be discerned through regular communication. The ambivalent nature of the symbol lies within its substructure rather than in the provision of the onlooker because it exemplifies how all communication breaks down, representing a simple articulation of what cannot be done, as everything is lost.

Alternatively, it may reflect a form of complexity that is so saturated it is unavailable to be communicated except through the use of a symbol. An example of this is a country's flag, which, due to its complexity, cannot fully articulate the entire Constitution or the full identity of that country. Therefore, it provides a form of signage to simplify that complexity.

In this context, the symbol becomes the last form of communication when all others fail. For example, in the case of cults or anarchist organizations, which are constructed in contrast to civilization, the symbolic nature of their communication emerges as the final form of expression because all other forms of communication have broken down, leaving no content to engage with. The symbol thus becomes the final emblem of communication.

This anthropological progression can be seen in the development of civilizations. It began with strong forms of symbolic nature to communicate what was otherwise unavailable for communication due to a lack of learning experiences that civilization provides. Early generations could not articulate the details of civilization itself. However, as civilization progresses, it begins to provide the symbolic representation of that complexity. When one looks back at this process, what they are doing is entering into its stage that constitutes a symbolic nature, not because the communication has become more complex, but because the lack of communication, in essence, marks the finality of civilization, everything becomes symbolic.

In a post-apocalyptic world, all structural elements of infrastructure become symbolic remnants of civilization, not so much to communicate details, but to communicate the last remnants of what once was, inviting others to engage in that communication, in the hope of remembering the bygone material.

An example of this process can also be found in child-rearing, where the initial stages of development rely heavily on symbolic forms, such as play, to help children understand the real-world elements these symbols represent. For instance, a toy car or train represents complex systems that a child cannot yet fully comprehend. The symbolic nature of play is required not because it contains complexity, but because that complexity cannot yet be communicated in its full form. As children mature, they no longer need these forms of play, as they have gained access to a more complex understanding and are able to function within the civilized world.

However, as adults, when individuals return to this form of play, it may occur in the context of recognizing their sentimental loss of understanding the complex forms to which this play represents. In this way, play becomes an attempt to reconnect with a past stage of development, almost like a rebirth of infantile stages. Now, they proceed as if they do not understand what they once did, in an effort to access that level of complexity once more. This is not a genuine return to the beginning stages of development, but rather a final effort to reconnect with what has been subliminally embedded in their subconscious.

The symbol then becomes ambivalent because of the lack of awareness of the participant, so that in one case it is the stage through which communication proceeds, and in another, it is the last remnant of that framework, beginning to decline right after the symbolic engagement. We could find this very enlightening in the case of electric lights, which both retain the symbolic nature of granting access to the entire scientific framework and civilization built upon the electrical grid, best communicating modernity and the connections that make up civilization, which is symbolic of a form of complexity that cannot entertain any other form. But in its ambivalent nature, it is also the case that electric light exemplifies the last form of civilization, being the last road before one enters into the desert or the small town that is disconnected, giving a sense of connection but actually marking the formation of the end. Especially in its simplicity, it becomes the criterion for the end of that form of communication. Thus, the scientific endeavor and the civilizational connection made up beneath it are bound to be in their last stage.

This is why lights at night are so significant in their simplicity. They present themselves with that ambivalent nature, but especially because they are the end of civilization, illuminating just before one enters the twilight, where civilization falls apart into the night. In some sense, there is the nature of the symbol, where the last remnant becomes more potent than the original, so that in the case of the flag of a country or state in decline, it becomes more potent as it becomes more degenerate in its construction. When a country is performing optimally, the flag does not serve as an illuminating symbol, but rather as the necessary banner that constitutes the generality of the state into a single frame.

The reason it is more symbolic in the case of decline has been hinted at above: the entire subconscious is laden with the details of that information. And based on all this knowledge that has been submerged to the point where the country is in a state of degeneracy, all that remains accessible to the symbolic framework compels this information to the surface of consciousness, warning of its degeneracy. For in the aftermath, the database will be lost from the subconscious as well.

It is extracting all that data in the admittance of its denial, as its last attempt to gain entrance into the consciousness sphere before it becomes submerged into a format that is no longer available for later conscious participation. This is found to be perplexing, for if one already understands the child at play and the adult that formats it, then it should not be the case that, at any point, they would lose that conscious development.

But in fact, it is true that any strong form of degeneracy, in which childhood play becomes a symbolic, sophisticated element, results in a finality: a deconstructed form of that latent subconscious material. Although it still remains in its very raw form, it has been corrupted to a point where it can no longer proceed toward the coherence that the symbol represents. Thus, the child's play loses its significance, in itself proving that information has no inherent interest in entering the consciousness sphere in the way a regularly developing child progresses from play to the structured form of that play.

The lack of interest itself has the individual unable to access the content from any vantage point, for there is no part of them that vitalizes such an endeavor. Of course, an analyst can perform that operation, but in the case of the individual it is lost, by the very inability to find a reservoir to interact with that part of their subconscious, so that in fact it is not lost, but cannot be accessed and is thought to the consciousness as a genuine loss, which in most cases would be.

Because of the ambivalent nature of such a condition, one cannot simply be the cause of degeneracy itself. When engaging with a symbol that represents degeneracy, one may not begin in a state of deficiency, but the interaction proceeds to provide that very deficiency. In the case of adults who re-enter childhood play, although it may not initially diminish their energy, if such play is activated without a formal context, such as employment or structured activity, it will eventually cause the information (that is only loosely tied to degenerative elements) to actualize itself against that framework. This process leads to the collapse of the very system that has once been developed.

A robust example of this is pornography. Although it may be enticing at various stages of sexual development, it is symbolic of the degeneration of sexuality through its format. In cases of high usage, it creates a formidable breakdown in sexual development, because one actualizes the symptom that represents the degenerate aspects of sexuality, thereby enlarging that criterion until they begin to lose a substantial portion of their sexual developmental capacity. This reactivates a modality akin to an infantile mind in relation to sexual concepts, despite any outward developmental progress.

If this is the theory, then the practical application is that high pornography usage would correlate with a degenerate form of sexual development. Intuition affirms this: we would not accept political representatives frequently engaging in that sphere, as we do not want the sexual degeneracy to translate into other arenas, especially where political competence is at stake.

This way is the simplest, though quite precarious, in its ability to restructure, since through its actualization it can disrupt its own form. We can even proceed to say that, in the case of high levels of complexity, or within a country at its prime stage of development, one constantly reactivates the symbol, such as the flag, and uses it as a form of actualization. In doing so, they degenerate to the informational database that correlates to that country, its civilized elements, and its substrates of consciousness. In this case, the flag becomes quite detrimental, for one could retract sizable portions of the psyche by actualizing this element.

It is not only the symbol that passes through this ambivalent nature, but any form of representing oneself or a community as a symbolic construct. Instead of serving as a representation that correlates to other conscious behavior, it becomes the very criterion of information itself. It could be that one is activating themselves or their community solely based on the degeneracy of the general public, rather than forming the emblem of the general framework. If one chooses to identify symbolically with a structured form, they will inevitably energize themselves through the degenerate aspect of that framework, whether they intend to or not, even if their interactions within it are based on a proper understanding of the symbol as distinct and complex.

For them to continuously actualize themselves as that symbolic nature, they must accustom it beyond the degeneracy of the framework. A clear example of this would be the class clown, who distinguishes themselves as the symbol of the degeneracy of that institution or class, making their entire nature the degenerate form of that framework; even if their engagement in that role is neither excessive nor overwhelming to the other participants.

There are multiple intersections between having an individual or group embody a symbol and other interactive locales, such as the interactive embodied locale. Although it would seem that a symbol is the culmination of interactive material encapsulated into a specific representation, and the individual embodies that culmination, this is not what occurs. Although we offered comprehension to the interactive embodied locale, which indeed remains aligned with a specific criteria of interactivity, such as a museum or a state capital, where interaction is both specific, non-negotiable, and embodied; this locale takes stock of one's already formatted lineage of consciousness, now open to the opportunity of integration.

An individual or group can enact themselves as the symbol, effectively utilizing either the degeneration as their modality to posture the proceeding framework, or encapsulation, where they contain the complexity to which has now the access through them. In the former case, they are not encapsulating any interactivity, and instead placing a negative contact of the contrast to that degeneration, but essentially embody the degeneration as well, just more so in a postured manner that would appear as though there is animation, no different than the illuminating lights preceding a desolate town.

If the objective is to appear as though it embodies the complexity, through which, now as an emblem, one can access that original framework, there is no coupling with that interactivity as proclaimed, for all resources are given to the succession of the emblematic notion, so that a general and wholesome picture emerges. In this way, it acts just like a country flag, which does not contain any material but reflects backwards to the database to which such material might be accessed.

This might fare similar to fame, or any representational figure, which we cannot argue are emblems to a certain framework and hence an embodied symbol. This is why it is particularly important to note the view of any symbol, or in our case the subjective perception of that embodiment. Although they are in fact symbols to a social criterion, they do not experience such in a fairly subjective manner. It is more typical to simply embody the representational aspect, so that an actor subjectively recognizes that modality in its formation of its representational correlation and the corresponding sociality. They usually would not take the direction of signifying themselves as an icon of that corresponding symbol. The reason for this is either to avoid the view that they contain all such information, that they have become the database, since it is bashful to retain such a perspective, or the alternative, where they follow the degeneration of that sociality, so that an actor may notice a masculine exclusivity that is symbolic in their nature, now possessing the sociality, but especially the degenerate aspects of a social landscape, to which they become emblematic and carry that symbol of its last stand before falling into the abyss.

They would require two elements to complete this transformation: one, the seclusion of that particular sociality aligned with their emblematic position, for in the inclusion of regular sociality, this would not occur because the symbol is not present in every social sphere. After the seclusion to that particular sociality, they must also isolate the aspects which the symbol embodied, namely the degenerate attributes. Therefore, not alone are they secluding a particular sociality but additionally the degenerate attributes that are successful at a campaign of provoking the symbol. They dwell in this degenerate landscape to provide the symbol of its last stand, or in the reserve of its downtrodden state.

For example, if a cultured person enters a small town, they engage only with refined sociality, severing themselves from the rest of the population, in addition to the degenerate aspects marking the town's decline. With these two parameters in place, they appear to embody the symbol of civilization, which stands in stark contrast to their identifiable state. Although this seems plausible, even natural, it is fundamentally flawed: the symbol of civilization is not an invocation of the town's civic framework, but a use of its last remnants to project a symbolic image. In doing so, they animate not the substance of civilization itself, but the very degeneracy through which it has been lost, serving as a reminder of its collapse.

All the while, it seems as though they carry out the bearing of civilization, when in fact their daily emblematic nature reflects its degeneracy, not in what is sustained or preserved, but in the sociality, they embody at this moment. Indeed, one becomes, in every respect, the living embodiment of the town's degenerate traits, the worst of them all, yet continues to animate themselves through the illusion of symbolic representation, which does little to halt the ongoing decay.

The sociality that they must embody is degenerating; even if they propose the opposite as a symbol. They must first become completely intact with that criterion to thus demonstrate their entire existence as an icon. In this way, the proceeding event is the full actualization of everything the symbol represents against, and after the fact, retaining a retracement of the alternative state as an exemplification of what not to be, not for sociality per se, but the very actualization that occurred from within. In each animation of that symbolic nature, they forgo more of that sociality in order to justify and align with the symbol; for a symbol without a sociality is not animated and is simply an object of existence.

This pattern can then work in perpetual motion until, that is, one does not have enough stability to exemplify the symbolic nature of the reverse and accepts their fate of participating in that sociality in all of their existence. In this way, in little time, one can perform a feat of degeneracy from which there is no return, and no psychological disturbance is required.

The objective for one to embody the symbolic nature of a framework of sociality can either be a mistaken psyche presumption or a determinate state of failure, to which this is the path of least resistance. Although there is the other effect, which reminds us of the ancient Pharaoh who sought to symbolize as an embodiment of that civilization, but was rather motivated, in the regular case, to catalyze the infrastructure under a rubric of possible interaction to secure that civilization, but in some cases, it was to secure a representation in a backhanded way.

Instead of sustaining a specific representational aspect, such as the role of king to a populace, it was used to encompass all possible representation, so that the very act of representing a role would discount that comprehension; and what was left was to symbolize themselves, to retract the interactive load of the populace by serving as a symbol: in a state of confusion, to retain all of that in a general format; or, in the state of purpose, to tally the entire experience of that development under a specific symbol, similar to the modern usage of a state's flag.

In the misuse of the psyche, one may presume that they are merely proclaiming themselves as a representational element, which altogether is not close to the dysfunction that comes from embodying the emblematic nature. But because sociality is controlled and the attributes are extracted in a septic manner, it is no longer a representation of anything but is symbolic of those attributes within that sociality. It departs from the realm of representation because it does not follow a continuum of correlation, for a symbol is not a following toward something but is an end in its design.

An advert is a representation because it reflects a greater comprehensive entity, while road signage is a symbol because it does not reflect a greater system, but encompasses a political and social framework within its parameters. There is no need for correlation in signage because it correlates to a framework by extracting to a generality, while the advert only represents and is not specific to a framework in which it ends its ideation, but rather is meant to continue onward; or the advert would not be effective. In this way, we understand a failed advert as being one that becomes a symbol, such as when it takes a political role, so that it does not lead onward to individual ideation but retains and contains all that is necessary for the generality of that information.

In other words, an advert and a representation are like a sentence, while signage and a symbol are like a statement. While a statement does extract from a database, it does not proceed toward one, whereas a sentence participates in an encompassing text. A statement is the prose of all the detail to which it correlates; it follows a specific sociality and extracts attributes from that sociality. A political statement would be the extraction of sociality that is considerate of that political framework, but also of the specific attributes which are considered for the construction of a statement. A statement will thus always be correlated to individual attributes, such as when one makes a statement, they are extracting a specific attribute of concern within a given sociality.

From the perspective of conversation, we can find exemplification of one's persona as a symbol, such that they will overcharge the degeneracy to which it makes impossible any form of retort. If the given parameters are correct, that is, that a symbol requires a determinate sociality that is secluded, and secondly, that it requires extraction from specific attributes but more specifically from degenerate aspects, then it is possible for one to embody the persona of a symbol and thus partake in a conversation. This would involve responding to another individual, isolated from any sociality beyond that specific criterion, and even going as far as to extract the degenerate elements from their material. In this way, in anything they would say, one could exemplify the moral aptitude that would be symbolic and in contrast to its degeneracy.

And because of the fault, the inability for one to complete their persona without degeneracy, it is thus always possible to be symbolic and contrast an individual as long as one secludes that individual from broader sociality and context; namely, the individual that proceeds before them is solely a criterion of interest that does not exemplify itself in broader context. One may then respond in kind to the degeneracy that underlies whatever their development is, so that they become symbolic in the reverse form: if it is a lack of humility, then the reverse symbolic nature would be one of posturing the notion and significance of humility. But preceding those events is the actualization required, in which they become the degenerate form interacting with that individual before they proceed to become an emblematic reversal of that and take upon themselves the role of the symbol in that conversation.

It would seem that real dialogue is thus impossible, and in truth there is no dialogue in any symbol; one cannot interact with signage; road signage, for example, for it ends in itself or in any other form of symbol, because it compacts but does not distribute. Thus, in dialogue, there is no dynamic in place: if one says one thing, there is no possible perspective of another thing, because the symbol distracts from the degeneracy and the sociality of that given notion, so that there is no response other than unavailability of speech or existence. In some ways, one loses full existence in the face of a symbol, because there is no way of interacting; and if the symbol imposes itself upon them, they lose the means of gaining entrance into whatever is extracted as the degenerate forms of being.

In the simple case of signage, road signage, although it does not seem like it is extracting degeneracy, it is, in fact, the emblematic nature of the deficiency in communication between state, drivers, and road usage, which all come together to extract the degeneracy to provide signage in that last attempt of generalization preceding the traffic light, which finalizes as a representing officer to fulfill complete direction. This is why the notion of roads and infrastructure in the post-apocalyptic scenario is always emblematic of the emptiness of civilization or humanity, for in that case there is no interaction henceforth, and it already remains stagnated and disruptive to individuality and personalization.

Auto is the exploration of systemic occurrences enduring current lifestyle, for the purpose of either exemplifying oneself, "take a look here, it might be valuable to you there", or to exemplify for the objective of contextually invoking the particular of current existence as if one were to reflect upon itself; to exemplify oneself for the objective of oneself, relying on social recognition to dictate, "it must be worthwhile of a study." The third intention is to take precedence that sociality is concurrent with one's alignment, to which they are displaying such sentiment from the vantage of personal experience of such setting.

Rousseau would be an example of the second criteria, and the one which is the basis to follow an autobiographical arc in both consistency for the individual and sociality. The first and third, to exemplify for social value, have no real objective for this piece of data in opposition to all other data, and it demonstrates that it is rather the further intention that other social value is less than such, for the centric experience is both universal and all-encompassing of a social function, to which one is thus coerced to expel the information for the betterment of reality. The third, that of sociality, takes a turn back upon themselves to recognize their participation, but ends in the same objective as the first intention by default of actively embodying that personal vantage point.

Biographical is the concern with a point of sociality, something of interest to public concern, that is made available from the vantage of an individual who takes up the task. The relationship to that specific point of interest can be the formation of an individual or representational connection, whether to have intimate knowledge or a vast sway of representational aspects. In this way, it is the same as autobiography, where instead of the focal point being oneself, it is oneself that is considered upon the projected landscape, that is, the element of interest.

Although it would seem like an abstract study of a criterion, the very amplification of noting a life or dynamic phase is for the production of a story and its narrative arc. The narration is instead the culmination in how one associates and intersects their own aspects to then play out in a formative journey of the other aspect. Josephus makes this clear; the absurdity of being a historian, for its only one's recreation of selfhood upon an external point of interest, and he very well made sure that his history was philosophized and laden with personal anecdotes, so as to perform a philosophical doctrine upon a narrative arc of history. Josephus is thus the aggregation of a story to dictate themes of courage, cowardice, and good and evil.xxvii

As long as the objective is a narrative arc, one who divests selfhood to its interest will imbue their own, alongside it, to then follow the metrics of an autobiography and its three motivations.

The imagined biography is one which is formulated as would a poet in understanding a theme without ever embodying that existence. It is to behold a subject as one's own, thereby allowing the process of biography to take hold.

There is another process: directly interacting with the representational system as if it were a speaking and intelligible being with conversational properties. This would constitute an interaction, although broaching on the subject of something altogether separate from individuality.

Take, for example, history, it is a story which precludes individuals. It is not individualistic, for it takes precedence towards a system that endows individualist notations but reformats them in congruence with complex sociality. For example, if an artist participates in known sociality, its art form is not their own in the sense of its individuality. The moment it participates in the social scene, it acts on its accord according to that system.

Interacting with it would be no different than attempting to interact with any representational element, and by virtue of one being close to the production does not bear any more individual access than one afar from its production. One does not understand the complexities to which their art is received, so that in any attempt at interaction, they are prowling a landscape that changes in every which way.

Even if we can attribute a core aspect back to the individual, this is of no consequence, for without the representational holding, there would be no recollection, either by sociality or the individual. One cannot believe their own art to be of any consequence unless they include a requisite projection of it being a participant within the representational spectrum. Art which does not fortify this criterion will not be acknowledged by any social being, as it would be considered part of infrastructure and not representing infrastructure.

PART 3: THE PARADOX OF PSYCHOLOGY

Chapter One: Psychology as the Axis of Personhood

A psychological analysis of a given scenario provides comprehension into a compartment of the structured psyche. This compartment is tangible as a criterion of personhood, as the developments in the field of psychology will continuously assert through different connotations. Generational trauma, for instance, will be a notation of personhood, whereas chemical imbalance or neurological discrepancies become another psychological approach to differ from that. Still persisting in the discipline of psychology because it seeks stable social cognition as the purpose of inquiry. The chemist is not attentive to bodily chemical imbalance, for they do not assert the notion that there is such a thing as chemical balance in the context of sociality. The absolute neuroscientist does not deem a discrepancy with an individual's social placement or lack thereof. The discrepancy will only be of interest to the functional system of the brain itself, despite its manifestation for normal interactive sociality.

That being said, we cannot assume that there exists an absolute chemist, biologist, or neuroscientist, for they do not contain a paradigm of balance within organic functioning unless they engage in a science of balance alongside biological function. We could say that an organism that does not decay in rapid succession is a functioning organism, but that is if we correlate the degree of decay to the social normalcy of that era. If higher life forms start to live double their age, then the biologist will assume a problem if an individual is under threat from that occurring, for their appropriation of the social environment is the metric for the notion of organic health.

The same can be said for the medical field in its entirety, with a virus or disease that is new to the social environment becoming a topic of medicine, while common viruses and diseases are accepted as factual nomenclature in the social realm and thus outside the field of medicine, e.g., for the doctor to offer societal advice against medical concern: "Why bother to worry? It is common."

Therefore, the study of medicine is the societal norm for what constitutes a varying degree of organic decay or decline. Thus, medicine is the attention to the social infrastructure, which makes it a study of psychology alongside that of medicine. Yet, medicine will not be as dependent on social and individual dynamics as we could say about biology and neuroscience. As long as the medical professional is somewhat attuned to the accepted and unaccepted elements of decay, they will be able to attend accordingly.

While the biologist who attends to the organism in its organic structure will always need to define what is to be considered organic and what is to be non-organic. If they did not have that criterion, we may be able to include every aspect of nature as being organic, even the actions of organic agents, and this will have the effect of becoming a study of everything and thus nothing. Instead, the biologist is going to assume what is to be defined as organic, and they do this by following society itself. When society presumes the molecular structure as organic because it happens without the interaction of humans, it may not always be the case. When the social environment heeds to the reproduction of molecular structure, they will identify that as a happenstance of human intervention. Each cell will be classified as a manifestation of human intercourse, without being able to be secluded as simple biological material of the universe. Notice that evolution is an important aspect of biological study, as it grants the appropriation of single sexual intercourse as being an element of cosmic movement, or in other terms: reproduction is natural while human actions are not. Human interaction with reproduction is biology's nemesis and can be handled if general society does not take interest in the sexual reproductive process as the primary interaction of molecular structure.

The neurological field must assume a normal cognitive function, and they spend their attention assessing processes of cognitive function more than the neurological aspects themselves. When the brain is able to communicate without the medium of personhood, it will become less dependent on psychology, but for the time being the reference point is the individual, with most being psychological symptoms and ailments; physical brain damage being the exception. We could even go as far as to say that neurologists are psychologists with the metric of the brain and its network as its point of reference.

We may want to differ by dictating that psychology is dependent on the fields of study insofar as they are dependent on it. The primary difference is that psychology attends the psyche without presuming to exclude psyche attachments to organic matter, while the others are not made clear to include psychology as an element of dependence. The reason being is that psychology is seeking the psyche in its entirety and accepts the network that the psyche is dependent on. The other fields are not psyche-focused but rather secluded to a discipline that has been conjured against the obviousness of psyche dependence. If psychology is doing its job thoroughly, then it will attend to the biological and neurological elements. When biology and neurology are proving their function, it serves to appropriate a more comprehensive approach to psyche study.

The connotation of generational conceptual frameworks is partaking in a complex web of family dynamics and child-rearing, while chemical imbalance is associated with environmental influences. Such that the perspective of chemical imbalance would be to conceive personhood in its chemical surroundings through its various channels to the body. It also is the case that it perceives the body in its organic state, or rather, personhood by its biological system. While the generational focus will be associated with conceptual frameworks that are not directly linked to the organism, to which themes such as forgiveness can be used, this will not be of assistance with a conception of chemical imbalance. Only the choice of chemical influences will be the antidote to rebalance the system, and nothing of conceptual interest will be concluded for that possibility.

Section One: Psychology and the Dynamics of Domestication

We find that psychology is fundamentally a form of domesticity, and for that definition, we will leave for another moment. But for now, we assume that it is not merely unassuming domesticity but rather an in-depth process of making aware a formidable source and domestication. Because of this, it is both productive and detrimental for the psyche and for social consistency. An overburdening form of domestication has as its side effect a realignment of the entire psyche system or is the realignment of the entire system. In either case, it constitutes a form of redirection, particularly if psychology takes on the task of actualization and deep domestication. However, this is not always the outcome; both the patient and the analyst may resist such a trajectory, precisely because of the problematic consequences or the existential implications it may entail.

Regular domesticity does not have the effect of conversing with source matter or existential material in the array of possible domestications but rather moves with the natural rhythm and direction of the conversation. Meaning to say, in the simple social interaction between individuals, which emulates in the mind of the individual, there is a dynamic between two sides of the conversation. When one says, "The weather is nice today," the other might respond, "It is possible that it might rain," or "I do not think it is as nice as you say," based on whatever prior claims or experiences they might have.

The point is that they are never going to reach a state of what psychology demands of domesticity, because there are a thousand and one dynamics required to reach that place. To have a conversation about the weather reach into the depths of one's childhood, even though it would still fall under the category of domestication, would require a constant exchange between two individuals, as well as a formidable context contained by the internal state of one's mind. It would require these conversations to manifest, even though they would not naturally do so unless prompted by an external circumstance.

For example, if one had an interaction with their parents that brought about a memory, this now requires a natural formation of that domesticity, because there is a social exchange between two thoughts: one thought is the perceptual experience of the moment, and the other is of internal questions based on early formations of memory. The memory is in a dynamical interaction with perceptual information, so that the outcome of that domesticated affair, whether in a single psyche or, if expressed, between two individuals, is a mediation between the two parts, and consequently a continuing social sequence. Meaning to say, the interaction with the parental figure has reached a culmination between that moment and one's earlier state, so that now there is an understanding to move forward based on that perceptual onset.

However, when domesticity is mined, as is often the case in psychology itself, then there is no exchange between one's current social bearings and the internal states being extracted. The only reason they are being extracted is due to a very robust context between two individuals in the clinical setting of psychology, or between oneself, if they have the ability to extract the information solely for the sake of healing or insight, rather than through a natural exchange that may occur.

For example, if one went to a friend and said, "Tell me about your childhood," or, "Tell me about your most painful memories," it would become a problematic instance, as there is no clear reason for the question, and therefore, the answer would likely not be forthcoming. And yet, if one is dealing with a troubling internal circumstance, based on perceptual interactions that lead back to formidable memories of their preceding psyche, then in engaging with it, there is a dynamical exchange within their internal state, but not within the social arena.

In this case, if one were to mention the plaguing thoughts that have arisen in their mind based on a perceptual instance, the other form of sociality contends with it because they do not contain an exchange with that. Why should they become sympathetic toward the other, toward such a deep emblem of memory, when that is not the context of their relationship? Just as one would not engage with a parental figure on the basis of those sentient memories, because they are perceptual associations, not memory itself. It would not constitute a dynamical interaction to have them serve as representations of the memory; rather, it is something that must be handled internally.

Therefore, it would be unusual for any relationship to take on the effect of mending the associations of prior domesticity. First, one needs to domesticate within themselves, between their perceptual information and the hidden details, and then a culmination may be brought into regular sociality, because now there is a dynamic reference point.

Chapter Two: The Paradox of Self-Esteem

The difficulty of not overgeneralizing the concept of self-esteem is quite significant because there is a criterion which is missed. This is the criterion that the conceptual realm is an opposition to the biological one, and without the differentiation we conclude as simplifying a matter that deserves the complex psychological analysis of its stature. Self-esteem is as easy to translate as its word choice; the self in perspective of the self. While the view of the self is a standard operation of psyche development, the self in social perception of the self is not a general function.

The psyche requires a homogeneous system, and appointing a self for that function would allow it to interact with itself from a seat that is both internal to the fabric yet separate to be chosen as a position of authority and reference. This is not the view of self for any other operation other than seeing an entity serve as a reference point. There is no esteem for that position because it is not a social reference point; it is only for the consistency of psyche interaction, which has somebody, anybody, seated as a lens to interact with the chaotic nature of psyche information. The psyche does not view that position as a respectable entity because it understands the transitory and arbitrary nature of its reign.

There is a social connotation to the self which has been appointed by the psyche that will be charged with the façade of the psyche in its interaction with the social environment. The psyche cannot position two selves, one being the reference point for psyche interaction and the second as the reference point for social interaction. It must occupy the same realm, even as the psyche finds respite in the countermanding of that occupation. It is only a matter of congealed psyche material which tends to become a distraction from the rest of the psyche. This occurs when it is assumed to be more than it truly is, taking on a certain stable ground.

When the congealed material enacts a position of stability, it promises more than it is; to be a seat of consciousness that will be of service in a hierarchy that will never fade. Treating the position as a hierarchical structure will have the adverse effect of losing true mobility within the psyche. Since a single position is chosen to reign, the rest of the psyche must be channeled through that, even as it becomes redundant and superficial. That is why we designated it to be congealed material, for it is a chosen clump of psyche-matter that happens to be placed together so a formation of a seated position takes effect; only to interact with the rest of psyche material that partakes in the culmination of a congealed space.

Congealed material does not serve as a very defined and potent reference for the social arena and will bear a contrary effect upon social manifestation. Because the self is viewed without the definition that would have the social environment pleased with a strict positioning, the self will begin to view the self with disdain, being meek in orientation. Thus, the congealed matter will cause the self to view the self as meek, as would the appearance of congealed psyche matter in the social environment. Yet, we have also noted that a psyche which positions alongside the promise of a stable and fortified ground will cause an immediate degradation of psyche development, being compelled to follow a specific pathway to enjoin any new psyche matter. It is also the case that this fortified position will appear in the social environment as it would seem, and thus the view of self will be in congruence with an esteemed representation of personhood. This is the paradox that we must unpack.

When the conceptual realm collapses and the individual falls into their own natural space, it will only follow that the positioning of self will be more straightforward and non-transitory. Without the appropriation of psyche movements, it will become an abridged version of its former self, and this would mean that the positioning within the psyche will align with the social environment. Since the psyche is fairly immobile within its system, the next available propagation of the psyche is the social realm.

The manner in which the social environment perceives an individual will be the identification and positioning of self. The self will move with social appreciation, without any direct control of personhood. The element of control will be the choices within the social arena, which will inadvertently have the effect of shaping their perspective of self, which will finally restructure oneself within the psyche. That change of position will be according to an esteem level, for the social environment only concerns this; to become closer to or further away from another social entity.

Therefore, the restructuring of the psyche position will not only be socially constructed; but it will also be diluted to the social prerequisite of a psyche position, its level of esteem. The position of the psyche is not for a newfound perspective of psyche matter but only for the sensitivity of a sense of esteem or lack thereof. This was the natural state of affairs in human evolution, as one had not the access to psyche movement. There was no other meaning for the position within the psyche other than a metric of social esteem.

Upon the advent of access to psyche movement, the position within the psyche became of utmost importance. Through the position arrives the allowance and distribution of psyche movement. The position becomes more about the advantageous perspective of psyche matter than its esteem for itself. We could term it humility, but it would be more appropriate to recognize it as a sacrifice for the ability to move within the psyche environment. By focusing on its esteem, the psyche will lose the ability to reallocate its material and thus disregard esteem.

However, the social environment will still perceive personhood based on an esteem metric because that is the most important element as it demonstrates safeness. Only those who have settled in this paradox will understand that esteem is not the only defining character, being that people must retain simplistic congealed matter to develop within the psyche apparatus. Therefore, they will perceive beneath the surface and follow whatever is manifesting to find whether it leads to material that is beneficial or not. This requires the willingness to release the evolutionary perspective of deciding action based on a mere representation and rather understand the complex realm of the psyche;

to have a weak representation for that very purpose. Thus, the social environment that has moved past the esteem metric will enable the individual to perceive themselves in a respectable position of complex psyche matter.

There is another problem when the perspective of the self is appropriated as being a simplistic matter. The psyche understands the difficulty of organic life, and when fronted with congealed matter as the representation of the self, it views a substance that will be unable to effectuate a response to natural organic strain. Because of this, the psyche will assume that the self is unable to respond to its organic structure and is thus a conceptual realm that is a threat to organic life. The entire mode of the psyche will be deemed a disease to the rest of personhood since it will not protect or affect organic life. It may also be the case that because the psyche views the social response to selfhood as meek, it will assume that one cannot adequately partake in the social environment, which becomes another perspective in how personhood cannot receive from the social realm for its organic needs, especially as it acknowledges the dependency for organic continuance.

We could account for the difficulty of the social environment, being that one can build a social environment that understands and respects this paradox, and seemingly all its members will both perceive the antiquated esteem of general consensus and the meek nature that a true psyche endeavor requires, and thus will not disapprove of either system. The self will recognize its own self as a respectable social entity, for there is appreciation for the material that it may unveil. However, we cannot convince the psyche that simplistic congealed matter will be appropriate for responding to the strain of organic life, as it is unavailable to the positioning effect to direct orders and be respected as an entity that will not move from its place.

We may be able to convince the psyche that a person in control of psyche movements, even if it may not be as quick to act to protect or persevere for organic life, will be deemed thoroughly superior in the long-term study of organic sustainability. We could prove to the psyche that more often than not, one who finds themselves in a positioned psyche space will move to action in the social environment against the overall picture, which will be biologically beneficial. Its very attachment to a certain position in the psyche and its overall fixation with the social environment's perspective of them will be the constant cause of social discrepancies, causing one to be unavailable to unleash their position or to disregard the social demarcation of that position, which will immediately threaten organic life.

We could even argue for this in the case of the internal organic system, for the position of authority in the psyche system will not be available to combat the complexity in the various elements of the system because it only sees its pathway of perspective. The one who will be generally equipped to handle the complex elements of their organic system is one who is positioned to be available to take various vantage points to handle the organic strain. For instance, the clear exposition of medical advancement would always prove that a conceptual development which led to medical science has the benefit of handling the nuance of organic degradation. While positioned authority which cannot follow the depth of medical science would do no justice for the nuance of the organic system.

In the social environment, we can argue as well, because the positioned authority in the psyche environment will become unavailable to diplomatic relationships and thus will always be at the precipice of detachment from social arrangements. There will always be cases where certain positioned actions will be beneficial, having found respite in their psyche for the immediate activation of a direct response; yet that is not the overwhelming situation which confronts normal organic life. We can easily argue that diplomacy protects and sustains organic social life and availability to all psyche elements will benefit the internal organic system.

This leads us to another inquiry, that of the position itself, which, having the stability and availability to direct psyche happenings, will be for itself.

Section One: Dynamics of Self-Depreciation and Sociality in Personhood

Self-deprecation may seem like a trait that only delineates the ego, so that one is either more or less genuine about their circumstantial psychological state, but instead, another manifestation takes precedence. Since we cannot shut down the psyche, self-deprecation will only be the cause of dispelling the intricate connections that make a wholesome experience of psyche experience. Through that depreciation, the psyche will now lose the wholesome state and will scatter amongst itself until a partiality of whatever detail, whether it is prior unconscious material or repressed conscious material, may take center stage. When we follow the process, we can almost assume that the modality of self-deprivation is not for the fulfillment of a pre-perceived idea that leads to depreciation but a captivation of a partiality of the psyche that will only be granted amnesty when there is a systemic depreciation.

Even more than this logical conclusion, in the extreme case where there is a seriousness that one takes in their psyche stance and thus personhood where depreciation is mostly avoided as being insincere or disruptive to the true state of existence, one will inevitably create a psyche environment in which they will be an emblem of depreciation.

Those psyche partialities that are never allowed the limelight will become so embattled that they will depreciate the psyche process, not by self-denigration in an outward fashion, but in a manner that is unnoticed, so that it becomes a subconscious process that slowly disassembles a social formation that is denigrable, which the psyche must respond to without any choice in the matter. If one's social experience is denigrated, the psyche will interpret it as genuine and will self-denigrate as if the sociality is performing the act, when in reality it was a backhanded move: the social stance was coordinated to be denigrable so that one would be coerced to denigrate, which then gives the partialities of the psyche their chance at that role.

Too much depreciation will give waywardness to the psyche parts regarding their ability to take control of psyche direction. Instead of following the normal process of integrating psyche parts into a wholesome and intact ego, this circumvents that process to give a chance to every vulnerability of the psyche. Since there are endless developing conscious particles inherent to a fully borne system, this can cause dissonance when every supplementary portion is given control of the present conversation.

Sociality becomes a very important part of ensuring that an extreme attachment to any of these portions does not take effect. When in depreciation mode, one expresses something that is not earnest to the wholesome nature of their system, but true in its modality. When this is brought into the social sphere, the opposing party, which can be a specific person or the general social system, will engage from the vantage of the opposing role. If a certain childhood vulnerability is being expressed, the other will ensure that the dynamic of that, mainly an adult voice, will keep the content in check. After much determination and reciprocation, one will be able to let go of their role in that psyche part, for sociality has shown another side of it. Sociality, on the other hand, will have gained a perspective of that vulnerability while still maintaining their vantage as the adult voice.

This is similar to what was mentioned above, where sociality can deprecate the individual through the subconscious, which has started the process, another method of having sociality create a dynamic that ensures that a psyche part gets attention, in this case, to not expend on that attention. The point comes to fruition: it is arbitrary but severe in the experience of role-taking so that it can be a learning experience for the psyche and thus integrate into systemic personhood.

With this dependence on sociality, if the opposition does not provide this much-needed dynamic inference, then one may find themselves rooted in that role and take the assumption that this is the whole nature of their personhood, when it is merely a psyche part that has taken advantage of a situation.

This can occur when there is either fear of reciprocating or responding, or if the opposition does not like their stance as counter-figures and instead chooses to side with the developing voice. By the nature of the opposition, it is not the learning side of the argument but is meant to provide a charitable act of allowing one to become wholesome again by virtue of contrast. Seemingly being the better choice as the role of the moving idea, the opposition may choose to opt out of the position and take upon that role themselves, relying on a more fringe part of the population, friend group, family, or any other sociality, to be that opposition.

Chapter Three: Contemporary Analysis of Good and Evil

Section One: The Organic Genesis of Evil

Conscious exposure via perceptual data when contrasted to the unveiling of the subconscious layers tends to over-proportion the conscious helm of deliberation, causing justification toward any direction. There is no fundamental evil, for there is a subconscious explanation of the sequence of events that are coherent and logical. The reason for social aversion is owed to the misappropriation of the subconscious realm that has been actualized into the conscious realm. The social agreement as to what should be tolerated within the conscious realm defines the notion of evil, and when this is surpassed, when the subconscious subtext begins to manifest at a higher rate, then mental and physical activity may constitute an evil premise.

This is why the unearthing of psychology, and its receptivity to all subconscious subtext, becomes the backdrop for an evil premise, for it sanctions the conscious realm with any detail of the subtext. It is not that psychology is attempting a paradigm that dispels the notion of evil, only that it follows the study of the entire psyche, within which the premise of evil fades from relevance. Especially considering psychology is the basis for providing subconscious justification to the conscious realm, which, in the case of evil, is the entire premise.

We could find within any action the sequential subtext that has provided leadership to its outcome. Having the sequential basis, which is the psyche acting as a mechanism that merely adhered to its objective, there is no determinate by which to judge the psyche as behaving in an uncharacteristic manner. Once character is established in its normal fulfillment, we are only at odds with character that appears out of place. Without something uncharacteristic to observe, to term an evil premise is to identify a disparity that is not organically justified.

The organic system that runs according to its character does not provide ample opportunity to define its structure as misappropriating its substances. Placing a conceptual premise upon an organic structure that seems to operate according to its themes would have the "evil" premise as a constituent associated with an identity, rather than a communal or common enterprise.

This is why we are almost ashamed of the associative elements of the term evil, for it seems deeply embedded within an identity system rather than a communal agreement. With its lineage of conceptual overlays (which do not apply to organic systems), the notion of evil has taken a turn toward being a premise that does not entail the universality of organic or communal systems. An identity is automatically actuated when the conceptual layer does not integrate into the organic system, not because this is the objective or mode of operation, but because what cannot be integrated takes the default helm of an identity. The specific identity then becomes an inhabited locale that is granted freedom from integration, as it constitutes its own realm and parameters of reality.

However, in the case of a conceptual notion of evil that does not integrate appropriately, the specific identity will be using a universal theme for its innate paradigm of reality. This confuses the terminology of evil, marking it as identity-bound rather than a universal notion pertaining to the organic system.

To make matters worse, as noted above, there is no fundamental evil, for the subtext is coherent, making the case for organic normativity. This would mean that every notion of evil is a communal enterprise, which approximates an identity by only a few degrees. It can be fairly difficult to distinguish what constitutes a communal enterprise versus what is based on a specific identity which merely fringes upon the commonality of sociality.

Moreover, the changes that occur in the communal sphere will dismiss former appropriations of evil, and those who continue with them will enter into the confines of identity. Thus, we have before us multiple reasons why the term evil more often is associated with identity rather than with the commonality of sociality.

We may wonder if there is any organic determinate that sanctions a certain control over the usage of the conscious realm in proportion to the subconscious. If we find that regulator, then we can recognize an organic system that defines the notion of good and evil. We must recognize that there is a limitation to subconscious material, for certain individuals will have exposed themselves to higher degrees of subconscious exposure.

What is not exposed, even to the subconscious realm, is to be considered unconsciousness and not an organic function of sorts. What is exposed to the subconscious realm is material that has a cogitation of the psyche to which a certain degree is deserving conscious attention. We cannot say that it is deserving full conscious attention, nor can we say to neglect the entirety of its substance, for it is an exposed element of the psyche and thus a component of the organic system, deserving its share of influence. It is up to the individual to identify the degree to which the conscious attention is perpetuated towards subconscious material.

On the other hand, we have a conscious realm which also has its limitations, for it should not expose itself to degrees of attention that would have its realm over-stimulated. We can agree that there is an organic function to having the conscious realm mitigated from stimulation, such that it can utilize its function in paying attention and not relegating the reciprocity of overwhelming substance.

Therefore, the limitation of the conscious realm is stimulation, conversely, on the other side is limited conscious attention. For the conscious attention does not appropriate material towards attending to the subconscious domain, and we can consider it to be at grievance with the subconscious realm, for it is not allowing that substance to take its normal effect into the helm of actualization. Thus, the limit of the other side of the conscious realm is a limited attention sphere to the subconscious material.

We have a degree in which there is organic function to conscious utilization of the subconscious material, and it is for us to decide if there is readily the same organic function in terms of its communication with each other. We can find evil that manifests from an over-stimulation of the conscious realm or an under-stimulation of its domain. Where either it attempts to the subconscious material against the backdrop of the normal attention sphere, to which the attention is diluted and the perception material is lacking; or where there is under-stimulation, where the subconscious material has no attention for the conscious helm, thereby having conscious direction which does not account for a major component of the psyche.

We can also find a degree of evil that constitutes the normal function of subconscious material. We could find evil manifesting from subconscious material which does not expose itself to conscious attention, where its material is now repressed. Or we can find subconscious material that cogitates at a higher degree than normal function, where it attempts its exposure to the conscious realm at a juncture where there is no solution other than the attention sphere to take effect with it. The exposure is to such a degree that the conscious attention, even as it finds no reason to attend to that level of interest, is necessary for the need to relegate those exposed elements which are threatening the stability of the system of the psyche.

We can perceive good and evil by its conscious platform which it has chosen or otherwise delineated from purview. When a platform of consciousness is attempted to be stabilized, what becomes of the next moment is the necessity of reintegration for a renewed establishment of differing and alternative conscious aspects. That next moment, which is not recognized, becomes an offset of the current choice of a conscious platform. While this is not evil per se, for consciousness essentials to be recognized for its relevance, in its continued attempt at relevance, all else will be sacrificed to continue that conscious aspect. Not only are all further moments and their necessities to become an offset, so does the entire history that has led to the conscious sentiment itself.

When conscious lineage becomes removed from the occasion, the only platform of consciousness becomes that aspect of fixation. Without its conscious source as a connection according to its potential for the future, what becomes of that aspect is a continuing offset of all conscious elements. While this is appropriate in the meantime, for there are intervals where such a direction is necessary, what commences is a repudiation of the substance itself.

Nature is directly connected, and when both the source and the futuristic potential are lost to its domain, what stands out becomes isolationist and begins to degrade upon itself. What begins as a conscious posture eventually loses its complexity and is left with a skeletal version of that structure. Only that which can be simply communicated and translated will continue, as when something dwindles, what remains are the elements of least resistance, which happen to be of least complexity.

This is why we often find that isolated consciousness begins to take on a political tone, as the individual or group starts to define all of their psyche elements in relation to that isolated aspect, and finds that there is a disagreement with the surrounding reality.

While they will posture their attachment to a conscious substance, they notice that the affairs of the political spectrum do not take a similar interest. Truthfully, they are modeling the happenstances of the psyche, for they notice that elements of the psyche are not in agreement with their isolationist consciousness, and they are only treating the political spectacle as the emulation of the vastness of their psyche. The reason they turn to the political realm instead of psyche elements is that they are benevolent to the fact that the political spectrum is the venerated reality to which, if there is a lack of alignment, then something needs to be fixed. Although, with their respect for the political process, which must be paralleled, the next step is recognizing that the political spectrum is only analogous to the wholeness of the psyche.

We could not determine evil as posturing consciousness, but rather as the full actualization of isolationist consciousness to the outcome of social injustice. The actualization of postured consciousness would consider that there is no other reality than that consciousness substance, and thus it must be activated on a personal and social level without the reprieve of detachment. In this context, evil is the manifestation of isolationist consciousness that will be actualized without any periphery available.

Alternatively, evil can be comprehensive consciousness that does not include its various elements, so that it would be the relinquishment of individuality for consciousness that would not include personal preferences. For the wholeness of consciousness does not find specific sacredness in the different formations of life, and the rock and human form are of the same pixelated substance, with no differentiation.

The loss of individuality in consciousness would have its enactment in the social sphere to be the removal of the entire social rumination, for when there is no individuality, there cannot be a social sphere to be respected. The truth of the matter is that this is not inherently evil, for consciousness that is whole is not missing any aspect for its actualization. However, because we speak from the vantage of an individual who must deal with their individuality, even as they presume to be attaching the wholeness of consciousness, their individuality will move stealthily and regulate that system. Yet, because they are delineating their individuality, what surfaces from their inherent individuality is usually of a very infantile arena, such as resentment or conflict of childhood, so that they will be galvanized for wholesome consciousness as if they were a child, and this is when evil manifests.

Infantile systems that adhere to a high degree of consciousness become another evil manifestation because they do not have the tools or skills to regulate consciousness. Consciousness by its nature enlarges the substance of interaction, and when the generation of that sphere is based on infantile measures, it will have a loss of complexity that is necessary for the consciousness system. We could all follow the pretext that nature is nature, only in pixelated form, and this may well be true for an individual who understands selfhood and intrinsic sociality, but it will be destructive for the infantile mind that does not understand that. They will utilize the notion of nature as just a pixelated form to justify their conflicting social aspects, to simply grant amnesty to move beyond all personhood anchors and resentment to follow this wholeness of consciousness. Furthermore, they may find favor in disrupting the social system as being a pixelated form of nature that does not matter if disrupted.

Although it is true at a high conscious level, that is only based on personal and individual development which leads to that consciousness notion. Preceding all the advances of the sanctity of individual life, one could not entertain the notion that all life forms are of a single pixelated thread, but once sanctity gave ascendance to this, one could follow that pretext. However, the process must still be adhered to, so that until one develops the sanctity of the individual, such wholeness of reality would be utilized as though an infantile form would take charge of a complex system.

Section Four: The Manifestation of Evil through Consciousness

There is a third manifestation of evil that is afforded to a utilization of dated elements of consciousness that were, at one point, novel aspects of personhood or groups. These conscious elements are not currently the rumination but rather are a part of the current process. These elements, because they are dated, would platform a juncture on a large continuum that would indirectly destroy further gains of consciousness. By returning to a preceding point on a historical continuum, every event after that juncture will be disrupted in order to allow the actualization of that consciousness.

Similar to the posturing of current consciousness against the lineage or production of its substance, which diminishes either past consciousness or its foundation in addition to the further possibility; this would do the same with current consciousness. While there is a justification for such deviation; because the element is found in the foundational base of consciousness so that it would not be so preposterous to claim that a restart would be amicable, by doing so they are destroying the succession of consciousness, and it will be even more destructive to gain at that juncture. While posturing current consciousness will have the effect of delineating its lineage, there is a process of growth that is deserving to detach from a foundation to allow for the full potential of the present moment.

The destruction is not with past consciousness but rather with the vulnerability of current consciousness, so that patricide is not most evil for destroying past consciousness but for devaluing current consciousness; the child as they are now. As well, by posturing current consciousness, there is the natural process of disconnecting from future potential and production because one needs to build their individual development before they pass it on. We accept the choice of putting off reproduction for the development of the individual, as there needs to be a developed individual for proper reproduction. The cost of the disbursement of potential is at the expense of current consciousness, for it begins to dwindle according to the potential of its horizon being continuously detached. However, in both cases, the expense of posturing current consciousness is within that consciousness and not against another juncture of consciousness.

The other manifestation of evil is when there is a reversion to prior states of consciousness, which instantaneously destroys the succession of consciousness after it has been actualized. In fact; it uses the vitality of current consciousness to gain access to past consciousness, for there is no ability to gain actualization of a memory unless we use a current model of animation. Thus, one is using current consciousness to retreat to a prior state of consciousness only to destroy the very consciousness that offers it animation.

The result is resentment toward current consciousness because one notices their dependence for retreating to an earlier stage. One finds that they cannot actualize earlier consciousness and perceive current consciousness as the culprit. In truth, they gain access to the "traditional" state only through the vitality of current consciousness, which deepens their resentment. As this continues, they sense that current consciousness reminds them of their emptiness, and that they have no true consciousness.

Current consciousness is removed from view, and the traditional state is non-existent, only bearing an attempted return. Thus, they feel pain toward current consciousness, for it is both their dependence and the reminder of their emptiness. This is the height of resentment, when one sees dependence as the cause of inner void. There is no escape but the disintegration of current consciousness, for they can neither be independent nor truly conscious. It is the madness of the child to return to the parent; the parent illusory; the child dependent on their own vitality to sustain that illusion and thus destroy themselves. This becomes the ultimate resentment: toward the parent for the falsehood, toward themselves for the act, and toward the child for sustaining and exposing it.

Chapter Four: Conflict as the Catalyst of Creation

The final creation, whether by genetics or otherwise, will follow the basis of the conflicting proponents that culminated in the newfound creation. This is prevalent as a criterion because, without the conflicting measure, it would be a similarity, thus not a creation, but rather an extension, though not by the terminology of extension, which is broader than its initial status, but exactly the same without change, thus not considered a continuation. The conflict is what provides the creation of something newfound that does not grant itself lineage back to the progenitors because it was created by the most dissimilar properties of each participant. Circumstances would not be entertained except through creative force or libidic energy that has been mended together, thus most dissimilar while being enabled as a form of creation.

Once we have established that conflict is the requisite for newfound creation, the level of development preceding the conflict arena decides in what manner the creation is a form of nuance rather than a chance mishap. Almost similar to the notion of one slipping, which cannot be constituted as a mistake or mishap, nevertheless is not in any proprietary form as a pedigree for development.

When the conflict takes place under the requisite of a mishap, which is the formalization of a rather underdeveloped creative format, the two agents, or in the case of a creative endeavor, the artist and their craft will follow. However, when the conflict follows a precedent readily available for the conflicting measure, it will proceed into a state of conflict and then replace the creation of the conflicting measures. Conflict, which is essential for creation, has been placed in a proprietary state, making the creation process as complex as possible.

Notes:

[i] Freud, S. (1911). Formulations on the Two Principles of Mental Functioning.

[ii] Plato. (1963). The trial and death of Socrates: Euthyphro, Apology, Crito, Phaedo (G. M. A. Grube, Trans.). Hackett Publishing Company. (Original works Apology, Crito etc., ca. 399 BCE)

[iii] Smith, J. A. (2018). Sunlight exposure and depression rates in the Northern Hemisphere. Journal of Affective Disorders, 234, 123–130.

[iv] Anglin RES, Samaan Z, Walter SD, McDonald SD. Vitamin D deficiency and depression in adults: systematic review and meta-analysis. Br J Psychiatry. 2013.

[v] Modzelewski S, Naumowicz M, Suprunowicz M, Oracz AJ, Waszkiewicz N. The Impact of Seasonality on Mental Health Disorders: A Narrative Review and Extension of the Immunoseasonal Theory. J Clin Med. 2025 Feb 9;14(4):1119. doi: 10.3390/jcm14041119. PMID: 40004649; PMCID: PMC11856923.

[vi] Sigmund Freud (1917). "Mourning and Melancholia," Standard Edition (on reflection and self-questioning after loss).

[vii] Parker, G. (2014). Melancholia: A Disorder of Movement and Mood. Cambridge University Press.

[viii] Smith, J. A. (2018). Sunlight exposure and depression rates in the Northern Hemisphere. Journal of Affective Disorders, 234, 123–130.

[ix] Arendt, H. (2018). The human condition (2nd ed.). University of Chicago Press. (Original work first published 1958)

[x] Hippocrates. (ca. 400 BCE). On the sacred disease. In W. H. S. Jones (Trans.), Hippocrates, Volume II (Loeb Classical Library). Harvard University Press.

[xi] Panksepp, J., & Watt, D. (2011). Melancholia: A disorder of movement and mood: A phenomenological and neurobiological review. Journal of Affective Disorders, 135(1–3), 1–17.

[xii] Panksepp, J., & Watt, D. (2011). Melancholia: A disorder of movement and mood: A phenomenological and neurobiological review. Journal of Affective Disorders, 135(1–3), 1–17.

[xiii] van Praag, H. M. (1993). Nosologomania: A disorder of psychiatry. World Journal of Biological Psychiatry, 152(5), 453–460.

[xiv] Oldenburg, R. (1989). The Great Good Place: Cafés, Coffee Shops, Bookstores, Bars, Hair Salons and Other Hangouts at the Heart of a Community. Paragon House.

[xv] Brooks, A. W. (2025). Talk: The Science of Conversation and the Art of Being Ourselves. Crown.

[xvi] Sigmund Freud (1917). "Mourning and Melancholia," Standard Edition (on reflection and self-questioning after loss).

[xvii] Jung, C. G. The Archetypes and the Collective Unconscious. Princetofn University Press, 1968.

[xviii] Walters, C. (Host). (2025, March 12). 120: Katie Quesada — Master storytelling with story expert

[xix] Journal of Affective Disorders. (2020). Unspecified article. Journal of Affective Disorders, 272, 116–124.

[xx] Irwin D. J. Brass, *Design for a Decision* (The Free Press, 1963).

[xxi] Once Upon a Time in Hollywood. Tarantino, Q. (Director). Columbia Pictures.

[xxii] Further examples — 'non-measurement', 'non-expressive-coloring', 'non-concern', 'hatred-of-representations', 'distaste, for-the-taste-of-society', 'shame', 'aggression', 'forced-sexual', 'anti-sexual', 'hatred-sexual', 'anti-masculine-feminine', 'feminine-sarcastic', 'masculine-sarcastic'. These examples are all representations which appear to lack the criteria even as they and society attend to them as such.

[xxiii] Plato, The Republic

[xxiv] Virgil. (1916). Eclogues (H. Rushton Fairclough, Trans.). Loeb Classical Library, Harvard University Press.

[xxv] Menninghaus, W., Wagner, V., Hanich, J., Wassiliwizky, E., Jacobsen, T., & Koelsch, S. (2017). The distancing-embracing model of the enjoyment of negative emotions in art reception. Behavioral and Brain Sciences, 40, e347.

[xxvi] Menninghaus, W., Wagner, V., Hanich, J., Wassiliwizky, E., Jacobsen, T., & Koelsch, S. (2017). The distancing-embracing model of the enjoyment of negative emotions in art reception. Behavioral and Brain Sciences, 40, e347.

[xxvii] Josephus, F. (Trans. W. Whiston). The complete works of Josephus (Book I §§1–12).